TVER ICONS

13th-17th centuries

ПОКѦIТЕСѦIE

БЛIЖБОСѢIЕ

СѢIНѢIНЕѮЖО

СѢКРАПКОВЕI

ГѢ҄ENѢIEКIXЪ

TVER ICONS

13th-17th centuries

Gennady Popov

AURORA ART PUBLISHERS · ST PETERSBURG

Selection, introduction and catalogue by GENNADY POPOV

Translated from the Russian by ARTHUR SHKAROVSKY-RAFFÉ

Designed by DMITRY ZHUKOV and ANDREI SHKORKIN

Managing editors RAISA KLISHAROVA and IRINA IVANOVA

On the frontispiece:
St John the Baptist. From a Deesis tier. Second half of the 15th century. Detail

© Aurora Art Publishers, St Petersburg, 1993

Printed and bound in Russia

Т $\frac{4903020000\text{-}999}{023(01)\text{-}93}$ без объявления

ISBN 5-7300-0492-3

"TVER IS OLD AND TVER IS RICH" goes an old Russian song. Yet fate ordained that for years, if not decades, this city, situated halfway between Moscow and St Petersburg on the River Volga, one of the main centres in North-Eastern Russia, was completely overlooked by Russian art historians.

In the nineteenth century there was a rediscovery of Tver's role in history and, to a limited degree, of its literature. In 1908 Academician Nikolai Likhachov published what is, in all likelihood, Tver's most brilliant contribution to fifteenth-century literature, the *Slovo pokhvalnoye o blagovernom Velikom kniaze Borise Alexandroviche*, written by the monk scribe Foma (Thomas). Yet in his review Academician Alexei Shakhmatov, while subscribing to his colleague's high appraisal, noted: "Scarcely... can one admit that Tver's cultural heritage amounted to much." Like many learned men of the nineteenth century he regarded Tver as a centre of secondary significance. It remained for Professor Arseny Nasonov, in his definitive articles — issued in 1926 and 1930 — dealing with local history and traditions of chronicle writing, to somewhat modify notions of the scale and intensity of social and cultural life in Tver between the close of the thirteenth century and the fifteenth century.

In the 1920s and later, several examples of fourteenth- to sixteenth-century Tver painting were restored and the illuminations in the *Chronicle of Georgius Hamartolos* were published, but most art historians continued to regard medieval Tver merely as a provincial centre.

Only new discoveries made by restorers over the past quarter-century or so, the organization of the exhibition "Painting of Ancient Tver" in the Andrei Rublev Museum in Moscow (1969—70) and the publication of a series of special research papers were able to shake the established view. It transpired that between the late thirteenth and fifteenth centuries Tver produced works of no less significance than Moscow and Novgorod. Tver's glory was by no means "illusory", to use Shakhmatov's word, its artistic achievements were shown to have played a notable role in the history of old Russian art as a whole.

1. View of Tver. Engraving from the writings of Adam Olearius. 1659

Although from the close of the fourteenth century the concept of a capital for the emerging Russian state was increasingly firmly associated with Moscow, only a short while before, a number of cities, with Tver by no means the least of them, struggled to dominate North-Eastern Russia.

Tver is first mentioned in chronicles describing events which took place in the second half of the twelfth century. As the thirteenth century progressed the name of Tver appeared with increasing frequency in annals. In the 1240s, a time of ordeal for Russia due to the invasion of the Tartar-Mongol hordes, the city became the centre of an autonomous principality, while towards the close of the century its princes chose a path of open resistance to the Golden Horde, looking to lead the movement to unify Russia's territories and re-establish their independence. Despite all the

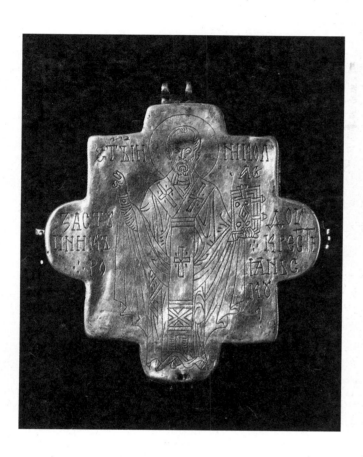

subsequent political and military setbacks suffered in the struggle for pre-eminence, throughout the following, fourteenth and fifteenth, centuries the principality of Tver continued to be second only to the Grand Duchy of Muscovy. In 1485 it was annexed by Muscovy, an event which represented a milestone in the formation of a united Russian state. No wonder contemporaries attached international significance to this development, relaying the information through diplomatic channels. Over the next two centuries, Tver, though no longer independent, retained its standing as a major centre, populated mainly by the merchant and artisan classes. Since the political lot of the principality of Tver was marked by a string of tragic events, many chapters in its cultural history, represented as they are only by solitary extant relics, lend themselves to study with great difficulty.

Indeed scarcely any thirteenth-century works of art have survived. Only the chronicles tell us of the erection of the Cathedral of the Transfiguration of the Saviour between 1285 and 1290 and its subsequent embellishment with frescoes. We should note here that this was the first time any work of art was mentioned since the Golden Horde's devastation of North-Eastern Russia between 1237 and 1240, a circumstance which may be taken as evidence of a definite revival in the principality towards the close of the thirteenth century. There was a renewed production of books, chronicles were written and there was a massive influx of people from the other ravaged towns in the region. The newcomers must have included artisans working in diverse trades, among them icon-painters familiar with the achievements of Vladimir-Suzdalian art in the twelfth and early thirteenth centuries.

2. St Nicholas. Obverse of a reliquary. Late 13th century or first quarter of the 14th century. Armoury, Moscow

Towards the beginning of the fourteenth century, along with Moscow and Novgorod, Tver established wide-ranging contacts with Byzantium, and not merely with its court. Thus, people from Constantinople (or Tsargrad, as it was known), Jerusalem and Syria came to live in Tver and contributed signally to its cultural life. At the town Monastery of St Theodore manuscripts were written in Greek, as for instance the 1316—17 parchment *Jerusalem Typicon*, now in the Vatican Library in Rome, brought there by the Greek-born Metropolitan Isidore when he fled from Moscow via Tver. Incidentally, this is but one of several scrolls in Greek that made their way from Russia to the Vatican Library. It is quite likely that the Monastery of St Theodore either had all Greek monks or a mixture of Greeks and Russians. At any rate authors in Tver were plainly familiar both with eleventh-century Kievan literature and with various Byzantine works.

Yet, despite the significance of Tver's contacts with Byzantium, its cultural development owed much to its ties with the territories of Western Russia, particularly Polotsk, and also with Novgorod and Pskov, which had not suffered so heavily from the Tartar-Mongol incursions in the thirteenth and fourteenth centuries, compared to, say, Kiev or the North-Eastern regions. Nonetheless, the heritage and traditions of Kiev, the ancient capital of Rus, affected Tver significantly in both ideological and cultural terms.

During the early stages of Tver's artistic development the traditions of Vladimir-Suzdal were particularly important, not surprisingly since prior to the Tartar-Mongol incursions, Tver had been part of that principality. Not infrequently the princes of Tver acquired the title of Grand Prince and maintained an official residence in Vladimir. Consequently court craftsmen had access to the treasures which had escaped plunder.

It was only logical that the traditions of the twelfth and early thirteenth centuries should be clearly reflected in the earliest artistic works of Tver provenance, and logical too that an attempt was made in Tver to revive the time-honoured art of coloured cloisonné enamelling. Indeed, the recourse to so complex an artistic technique during the period under the yoke of the Golden Horde is both remarkable and curious, since in the eyes of contemporaries enamelling was viewed primarily as a metropolitan art form.

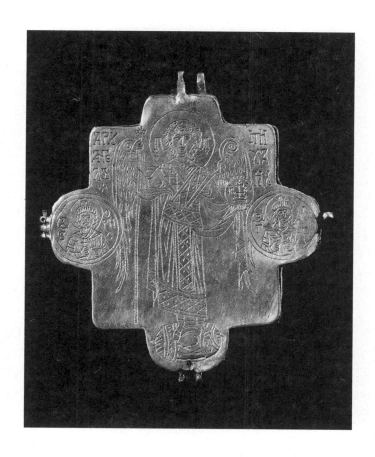

The influence of metropolitan Vladimir can be seen in one of the oldest extant items associated with Tver, a reliquary from the late thirteenth century or first quarter of the fourteenth century (ills. 2, 3), its surfaces decorated with the engraved figures of St Nicholas and the Archangel Michael, and medallions enclosing half-length portrayals of Russia's first saints, the martyred princes Boris and Gleb. It is quite possible that this reliquary was owned by Mikhail Yaroslavich, the Grand Prince of Tver (1271—1318), whose reign was marked by major events in the city's cultural and artistic life.

The most striking example of early Tver art is the illuminations in the parchment *Chronicle of Georgius Hamartolos*, 129 in all, of which some twenty were added later, either at the end of the fourteenth century or at the beginning of the fifteenth. Its first part was written in Byzantium in the ninth century by Georgius Hamartolos and the text was continued by an anonymous hand in the tenth century. Most scholars believe it was first translated into Slavonic at the court of Yaroslav the Wise in Kiev in the mid-eleventh century. At about this time the illuminations must have been copied from the Greek original. However, it is still not clear what manuscript the Tver artists used to make their copy. It was evidently not the Kiev copy, but one produced later, possibly in Vladimir in the twelfth or early thirteenth century.

The text of the Chronicle begins with the creation of Adam and incorporates a wide range of stories and events from the Bible and from ancient and Byzantine history. It is possible that the Tver manuscript may have been intended to introduce a series of illustrated local chronicles, but this is hard to judge since the last chapter is missing. At any rate the concept of an elaborate, partly or fully illuminated, chronicle setting out local events within the context of world history could have originated only during the period of Tver's rise, in other words, during the reign of Mikhail Yaroslavich. Palaeographic evidence, however, confirms a later dating, and we must take into consideration the fact that work on the illumination of the *Chronicle of Georgius Hamartolos* was interrupted.

The specific artistic features of the illuminations attest to a diversity of artists working in Tver during the first decades of the fourteenth century and demonstrate the high overall level of their skill. The manuscript begins with two full-page frontispiece miniatures (ills. 4, 5), the first depicting Christ enthroned with the Prince Mikhail of Tver and his mother Xenia interceding, the second portraying the author of the Chronicle, Georgius Hamartolos the Sinner, occasionally known simply as Georgius the Monk. The other illuminations in the manuscript (ills. 6—12) illustrate the text.

Though traditionally handled, the two frontispiece illuminations are grandiose, expressive and rich in ornamental motifs, while the characters are well delineated. Note also the exceptional significance attached to partnering of the prince's portrait with that of the Chronicle's author; this tradition derives from manuscripts produced in Byzantine scriptoria and from early eleventh-century Kievan miniatures. The first illumination probably served as the prototype for many later imitations. In fact, one later Tver icon (Cat. Nos. 180, 181) is, in effect, a variant of the Chronicle miniature, the sole difference being that in the icon the prince and his mother hold a model of the city of Tver which is in their protection. A typological affinity can be seen in the last icon published here (Cat. No. 182), portraying the Prince with Bishop Arsenius.

The first illumination is signed by Procopius, who was also the author of the second frontispiece and the two succeeding miniatures within the text. It is possible that this outstanding master may have supervised the whole of the manuscript's illumination. At any rate the other miniatures were executed by at least nine different painters. Some manifestly adhere to the artistic traditions of North-Eastern Russia, and we can discern here borrowings from Vladimir-Suzdalian art (ills. 8, 9), while others reveal links with Western Russian traditions (we have already mentioned Tver's contacts, particularly with Polotsk). Some illuminations towards the end echo Novgorodian art of the late thirteenth century and first half of the fourteenth (ills. 7, 11, 12); at that time master craftsmen from Novgorod may have been working in Tver. Indeed, both at the turn of the fourteenth century and later large numbers of artisans from other places settled in Tver and their skill and creativity formed the groundwork for the emerging local traditions. This is superbly illustrated by the Hamartolos Chronicle illuminations; therein lies their main significance.

The oldest icon associated with Tver, that of SS Boris and Gleb (Cat. Nos. 1—5), may be dated between the second half of the thirteenth century and the first third of the fourteenth. Like other known early works, it is also, no doubt, the copy of an earlier prototype.

The energy and power that radiate from the figures portrayed reflect the period during which the icon was painted, a time of dramatic upheavals, of tragic devastation wrought by the incursions of the Golden Horde. This was also a time of mounting resistance, of hope of liberation in a bitter struggle for independence. The two saints, Boris and Gleb, became a symbol of their age. Though the poses are virtually identical, with each holding a cross in his right hand and a sword in his left, the figure of Gleb possesses a gentler outline, whilst his elder brother is more massive and angular. The subtle difference echoes the characterization of the two brothers in such eleventh-century literary works as the *Homilies from the Lives of the Saints*, *Legend* and the chronicle *Tale of the Murder of the Holy Martyrs Boris and Gleb*.

The icon-painter's work is clearly still bound by earlier traditions, which determine all the basic features, such as the symbolical poses and gestures, the exaggerated scale and the conventional treatment of the forms. Drawing inspiration from archaic sources, the painter produced an impressive work which, along with the finest illuminations of the *Chronicle of Georgius Hamartolos*, illustrates well the advances made in Tver painting at the time when it was still assimilating a vast artistic heritage and evolving an artistic standard of its own.

The saints' garments are richly patterned and studded with precious gems, revealing the impact of court tastes. The icon is further enriched by inset gems on the haloes and sword handles, while the ornamentation of the fur-trimmed hats, the traditional headgear of Russian princes, clearly echoes the patterns of eleventh- and twelfth-century Kievan cloisonné enamels. Originally the figures were set off against a silver ground, now almost completely missing. The decorative richness of the icon is above all symbolical, bearing witness to the great merits of the two brothers as protectors of their motherland.

The cult of SS Boris and Gleb was possibly not simply the result of Vladimir-Suzdalian tradition, for the martyred princes were also extensively revered in Western Russia, and more specifically in Polotsk, with which, as noted above, Tver had active cultural links; we should mention that Tver's first ordained bishop, Simeon (died 1289), came from Polotsk.

The richness of this icon was appreciated from the very first. It was repeatedly renewed, the earliest such renovation dating back to the first third of the fourteenth century, when the Cathedral of the Saviour, where the icon was most likely kept at the time, probably underwent repair. The faces were remodelled using expressive highlighting; Boris's face has more contrasts and is more full of energy, whilst Gleb's visage is again gentler, with soft transitions from light to dark. This emphasizes the "beauty of youth", about which so much is written in literature devoted to the murder of the two saints. Whereas Gleb has an inner intensity, Boris appears to be wiser and more tranquil. The handling discloses a familiarity with the latest trends, which emerged in Balkan icon-painting of the turn of the fourteenth century. At the same time, the novel modelling of the icon's second layer, along with the pronounced graphic quality and expressiveness of most of the illuminations in the *Chronicle of Georgius Hamartolos*, point to the development of local aesthetic ideals and artistic traditions.

The evolution of a local school of painting was, however, interrupted, or at least suspended, by political developments. In 1318 Prince Mikhail Yaroslavich was put to death by the Golden Horde, which, less than ten years later, in 1327, quashed a major rebellion in Tver with great severity. Only towards the middle of the century

4. Master Procopius. Christ Enthroned with Interceding Prince Mikhail Yaroslavich of Tver and Princess Oxinia (Xenia). First frontispiece illumination from the *Chronicle of Georgius Hamartolos*. First third of the 14th century. Russian State Library, Moscow

5. Master Procopius. Georgius Hamartolos. Second frontispiece illumination from the *Chronicle of Georgius Hamartolos*. First third of the 14th century. Russian State Library, Moscow

6. The Great Pharaoh,
Progenitor of the
Egyptian Pharaohs.
Illumination from the
*Chronicle of Georgius
Hamartolos.* First third
of the 14th century.
Russian State Library,
Moscow

was some degree of artistic revival possible. These years witnessed the writing of
the *Good Measure*, a parchment scroll with the text of a legal code which was popular in old Russian society. Though its decoration (ill. 13) is very modest, indeed
somewhat provincial, its production involved a number of scribes, most of whom were
of West- or South-Russian origin, bearing witness to the existence of a large scriptorium. In the eyes of contemporaries Tver remained a major seat of culture, as is
indicated by the steady influx of master-craftsmen.

Chronicles record in the 1340s and 1350s a consistent campaign of embellishment
of the Cathedral of the Transfiguration, commissioned by Bishop Fiodor (1344—
1360; died 1367). The detailed list of the varied jobs undertaken shows that Tver
still had several jewellers' and painters' ateliers, as well as a small artel of masons.
The level of the work is indicated by the Cathedral's copper gates, executed in 1344—
45 or 1357, with an engraved scene of the Old Testament Trinity. The virtuoso use of
metal-working techniques gave a sense of space, plasticity and movement. In this
respect the scene can compare with the finest examples of fourteenth-century Muscovite jewellery, although there is a hypothesis suggesting their Novgorod origin. In
the sixteenth century Ivan the Terrible commanded that the gates be taken to
Alexandrova Sloboda, in what is today the town of Alexandrov near Vladimir.

The famous *Fiodor Lectionary* (ills. 14, 15) was almost certainly produced in
Tver during this period. For many years the manuscript was dated to the thirteenth
century and was associated with Prince Fiodor (Theodore) Rostislavich the Black of
Smolensk and Yaroslavl. Later scholars tended to date it to the second or third
quarter of the fourteenth century, holding that it originated in one of the larger
centres of North-Eastern Russia. We may take the centre in question to have
been Tver and suggest that the manuscript was commissioned by Bishop Fiodor.
At the beginning of the manuscript are two sumptuous illuminations, the first of
which portrays St Theodore Stratilates in military dress. The inclusion of such a picture in a lectionary is unique and we may assume that it reflects the express command of Bishop Fiodor, whose namesake the saint was. It is also worthy of note
that Tver was the site of the large, deeply revered Monastery of St Theodore and
the lectionary may have been destined for that very establishment.

7. Life of the Rachmans. Illumination from the *Chronicle of Georgius Hamartolos*. First third of the 14th century. Russian State Library, Moscow

The two frontispiece illuminations and the wealth of ornament betray a familiarity on the part of the artists with the leading trends in fourteenth-century art. The manuscript also has three miniatures portraying the Evangelists, which were painted at an earlier period and inserted here. Their style echoes the artistic tradition of the thirteenth century, and displays an affinity with the illuminations in the *Chronicle of Georgius Hamartolos*. The main, best part of the illuminations was evidently the work of a visiting artist.

The afore-mentioned gates of the Cathedral of the Transfiguration and the illuminations in the *Fiodor Lectionary* demonstrate the high standards reached by local artists, thus countering the view that there was a marked decline in Tver's artistic development during the middle and second half of the fourteenth century, and that Tver was at that time a mere provincial town. On the contrary, Tver artists were evolving and finalizing their own particular style and school in this period.

The oldest icon to reveal marked local features is that of *Christ Pantocrator* (Cat. Nos. 6, 7), which displays a curious blend of expressiveness and static immobility. The half-length figure, painted in a combination of muted tints for the figure itself and vivid orange-reds on the binding and edges of the book and the yoke of the chiton, stands out against the light-toned background, creating the impression of an accentuated relief. Form is delineated by means of strong highlights and clearly etched white strokes. In comparison with the *SS Boris and Gleb*, the *Christ Pantocrator* is more conventional and is based on a more ornamental approach. The garments are modelled by means of straight lines, with virtually no glazing or halftones. The style reveals a blend of diverse elements derived from earlier artistic traditions and new trends stemming from the so-called Paleologue revival in Balkan icon-painting, along with the flatness and clarity that were inherent in fourteenth-century trends.

The power of the image, its inner fire and individualized interpretation illustrate well the distinctly defined range of ideas that dominated Tver in the middle and second half of the fourteenth century. The asceticism is not accidental, but is a trait that emerges at times of political and economic decline in feudal societies. A similar development could be observed in Tver's spiritual and intellectual life.

8. Angel Leading
Moses into the Promised
Land. Illumination
from the *Chronicle of
Georgius Hamartolos*.
First third of the 14th
century. Russian State
Library, Moscow

Throughout the second half of the fourteenth century the princes of Tver strove to acquire allies in their struggle against Moscow, to which end they addressed themselves to both neighbouring Lithuania and distant Constantinople. In 1375, however, they were gravely defeated by the united forces of the Russian principalities under the command of the Grand Prince of Moscow, an event which decisively influenced local cultural development, practically up to the end of the fourteenth century, determining the archaic nature of its colouring.

Icons similar to the *Christ Pantocrator* were by no means few and far between. On the contrary, they formed the basis of a definite trend in Tver painting with a set of consistent features: a characteristically conservative approach to modelling and colouring; rigid, two-dimensional, seemingly petrified forms; the predominance of a whitened range of cold and muted tints; an exaggerated intensity in the portrayal of figures. This trend prevailed right up to the sixteenth century.

These features are particularly clearly seen in a small icon of the *Archangel Michael* painted at the turn of the fifteenth century (Cat. Nos. 8, 9). Despite the evident provincial traits, the iconography suggests the artist's possible familiarity with works influenced by Paleologue traditions. The icon's patronal association with the two princes of Tver earlier mentioned, Mikhail Yaroslavich and Mikhail Alexandrovich (1368—1399), proves that it could not have been painted in the outer regions of the principality, making the elements of provincialism all the more striking, contrasting as they do with the majestic pose and the deep iconographic concept of a prototype to which the icon-painter so faithfully adhered. Though this unknown but undoubtedly stylistically high prototype is recreated in the Tver icon on a folkloric level, the painter has produced a striking image full of inner power.

The *Archangel Michael* furnishes virtually the sole indication of a notable slackening in Tver's artistic evolution as a result of the adverse political conditions during the second half of the fourteenth century, notably the devastating incursions of the Golden Horde and the setbacks in the struggle against Tver's principal political rival, Muscovy. By the close of the fourteenth century, however, the archaic features still seen in this icon, which hark back to the formation of a local culture at the turn of the fourteenth century—a time marked by the idealization of the traditions that

14

existed prior to the Mongol-Tartar invasion — no longer dominate the overall picture. We now witness a new phase of Tver's cultural and artistic rise that reached its culmination in the mid-fifteenth century.

For the principality of Tver the last two decades of the fourteenth century were a time of relative peace. The writing of chronicles resumed and construction in stone increased not only in Tver itself, but also in the principality's second largest city of Staritsa and in Tver's neighbouring fortress of Gorodnia (or Verziatin).

From 1399 on, the interiors of newly built structures in Tver and Staritsa were decorated with painting. Obliterated in the process of subsequent reconstruction, the only idea we have of them today derives from excavations conducted in the early years of the twentieth century, for example in Staritsa, and from the discovery and restoration in the 1970s of fragments of wall-paintings from the Gorodnia Church of the Nativity of the Virgin (ills. 23—25), broken up when the church was renovated in the eighteenth century. Still, these few remnants do provide us with some idea of Tver painting during the first quarter of the fifteenth century.

Most new construction and artistic undertakings, including the commissioning of manuscripts, were initiated by Tver's episcopal see which, from 1390 to 1409, was headed by the Bulgarian-born Bishop Arsenius, an associate of the Metropolitan Cyprian of Moscow. Under the Bishop's supervision Tver also established active ties with the cultural world of the Balkans. Indeed, interest in the artistic traditions of the Balkans greew apace in Russia during the second half of the fourteenth and early fifteenth century along with the strengthening of its own national traditions, and in this respect Tver was no exception. Written sources illustrate well the nature of the developing relationship with the Balkans, showing a tendency to idealize the city's contacts with Byzantium in opposition to its ties with Muscovy. This reflected Tver's persistent rivalry with Muscovy, which now moved out of the purely political world into the cultural and intellectual domain. The idealized view of the Tver principality's role in world history is clearly expressed in the mid-fifteenth-century *Paean to the Pious Grand Prince Boris Alexandrovich*, ascribed to the Monk Foma. Particular emphasis was placed on the piety of the princes of Tver and on the services that they had rendered to the Orthodox world as a whole.

9. Life in Exile, in the Hide of a Lion, of King Nebuchadnezzar of Babylon. Illumination from the *Chronicle of Georgius Hamartolos*. First third of the 14th century. Russian State Library, Moscow

15

The interest evinced from the late fourteenth century in Byzantine and Balkan art in Tver derived from the fascination with the progressive trends associated with the Paleologue revival. Local artists could also learn from the splendid Muscovite and Byzantine icons brought to Tver by monks of the Trinity-St Sergius Monastery on their flight to escape the ravages of the Golden Horde in 1408. One of these monks was Epiphanius the Wise, a leading medieval Russian writer, who brought with him a Gospel book, as we learn from an *Epistle* (1414—15) that he addressed to Kirill (Cyril), the abbot of one of Tver's monasteries. Its illuminations were the work of Theophanes the Greek, originally from Constantinople, the most illustrious of all artists at the turn of the fifteenth century. Local imagination was particularly excited by the miniature depicting the Hagia Sophia in Constantinople.

From the end of the fourteenth century contacts with Mount Athos, a major centre of Greco-Slavonic cooperation, were of great significance for cultural life in Tver. During the first third of the fifteenth century many scribes from Tver worked in the scriptoria of Athos monasteries, especially the celebrated Lavra of St Athanasius, and it is also possible that Tver painters visited Mount Athos, no doubt due to the sponsorship of Bishop Arsenius and the Metropolitan Cyprian. We should note that the latter helped to augment the library of the Tver see with fresh translations.

Despite new cultural links and sources of influence, however, Tver retained an interest in its own past, its monuments recalling the 'golden age', when the thriving city had played a leading political role. This continued interest is reflected in the way the early history of Tver is presented in local fifteenth-century chronicles.

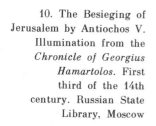

10. The Besieging of Jerusalem by Antiochos V. Illumination from the *Chronicle of Georgius Hamartolos*. First third of the 14th century. Russian State Library, Moscow

It must have been no later than the first decade of the fifteenth century that efforts were made to refurbish the ancient manuscript of the *Chronicle of Georgius Hamartolos*, work upon which had probably been interrupted in 1327. Once again the initiative came from Bishop Arsenius. Several miniatures were painted and various sections revised or supplemented, most likely in preparation for the production of a new copy of the text (possibly that now in the Hermitage Library in St Petersburg).

The new miniatures were to compensate for the hiatuses and impart a sense of completeness to the Chronicle. The five or six illuminators involved in the work on the Chronicle produced a total of twenty-two miniatures, and in the absence of the older original they naturally re-invented many of the episodes needed, introducing many specifically Russian genre details. Though the new miniatures are not of an even standard, they were definitely executed by painters, not by professional draughtsmen. Most have a generalized black contour painted in with a brush over the initial drawing. The colouring is vivid, the tempera laid thickly with broad brush-strokes (ill. 16). Form is often indicated only roughly. The more interesting of all the miniatures is that depicting the Prophet Daniel being led out of the lions' den (ill. 17). The draughtsmanship here is fine, while the colour scheme consists of a subtle play of brownish oranges, pinkish purples and greyish blues, which serve to create a rich colouring. We clearly see the painter's wish to entertain by pictorially reproducing the text in fullest detail. The artist must have been well acquainted with the fourteenth-century tradition.

Unfortunately, the paint layer of the Chronicle's later illuminations has flaked away in many places. To judge by the many additions and marginal drawings the Tver copy excited great interest not only in the fourteenth century but also in the fifteenth and sixteenth centuries and even later, which could not but affect its overall condition. Heavily dog-eared, its restoration was completed in 1983 only after many years of painstaking work.

It is possible that by the early fifteenth century Tver illuminators had forgotten the art of painting on parchment, as from the close of the fourteenth century the use of paper had become widespread. Still, parchment continued to be employed along with paper, though to a lesser extent, not only in Tver but also in other centres.

One of the rare locally produced parchment manuscripts from this period is the 1406 copy of the *Patericon of the Kiev Monastery of the Caves* (ill. 18), specially commissioned by Bishop Arsenius, who personally revised the thirteenth-century Kievan text. The decoration is unassuming and comprises headpieces of the so-called Balkan type, plus several cinnabar headings and initials.

The ornamentation of this commissioned codex would appear to be surprising in view of the heavy revision required in its preparation, but this ascetic approach is characteristic of Tver art at the turn of the fifteenth century, when, as a result of the political upheavals and internecine strife between local rulers, it fell to the bishopric to act as chief sponsor and patron.

Only later do we perceive a tendency towards the production of more varied and richly decorated manuscripts. Thus, in the 1417 Gospel book (ill. 19) the ornamentation is complex and highly individualized. The headpieces combine a fanciful blend of various types of embellishment, from Byzantine vegetable motifs and neo-Byzantine Balkan interlace to already-dated teratological motifs (in the initials), giving this heavily ornamented and gilded manuscript a highly uncommon, even contradictory, character. The variety of elements, found at the root of this or that work of art, would appear to be characteristic of the initial phase of this new upsurge in Tver culture, and it is not surprising if one takes into account adverse conditions during the second half of the fourteenth century.

A similar phenomenon, but this time with respect to architecture, can be seen in the contemporary white-stone Church of the Nativity of the Virgin in Gorodnia (ills. 20—22). The imposing façade and sweeping architectural scale — at one time the building was enclosed by a gallery — are not complemented by equal clarity in the structural concept of the interior. In some of the architectural elements, such as the minutely carved details of the portals, we may discern what is conceivably the impact of the applied arts, and some of the decorative motifs, particularly the trefoil-headed windows on the southern side, manifestly recall such items as folding metal icons, pyxes and reliquaries.

The imposing scale of the structure and the intimate nature of the various details impart an inimitable beauty and individuality to the building. As in the headpieces

11. The Dream of the Emperor Constantine the Great. Illumination from the *Chronicle of Georgius Hamartolos*. First third of the 14th century. Russian State Library, Moscow

12. The Translation of the Body of the Emperor Julian the Apostate. Illumination from the *Chronicle of Georgius Hamartolos*. First third of the 14th century. Russian State Library, Moscow

of the 1417 Gospel book, we distinctly discern the explicit desire of the local craftsmen to create their own stylistic versions through the interaction of artistic impulses and impressions different in their sources gathered from various art forms.

Unfortunately, only few early fifteenth-century Tver manuscripts survive. The Gorodnia church appears to be the sole tangibly extant example of early Tver architecture, all other fourteenth- and fifteenth-century structures being known only on the basis of archaeological evidence.

Gorodnia, otherwise known as Verziatin, was a Volga fortress on the road to Moscow. The Church of the Nativity was erected in the late fourteenth and early fifteenth centuries, but after a conflagration in 1412 the upper section was completely rebuilt. Thus the present building may be dated to the second or beginning of the third decade of the fifteenth century. The interior was decorated with wall-paintings shortly afterwards. What has survived of these paintings,

13. The Righteous Measure. Middle or third quarter of the 14th century. Russian State Library, Moscow

however, can be found for the most part in the chancel and on the window jambs of the upper tier. Most of the frescoes were destroyed in the eighteenth century and only a few fragments have been uncovered in the process of restoration. These have been painstakingly pieced together and mounted on a new ground, and it is now possible to study them. Beneath the plaster restorers also discovered a large number of preparatory drawings (ill. 24).

This unique extant group of early fifteenth-century wall-paintings (ills. 23, 25) thus serves as a point of departure for assessing the evolution of the visual arts in Tver during the medieval period.

Close study reveals great advances in Tver painting during the first decades of the fifteenth century, disclosing a very distinct interest in the dominant artistic traditions of the day. In Tver, under conditions of continued conflict with Moscow, tendencies that were characteristic of Russian culture as a whole in the fourteenth and fifteenth centuries acquired specific traits. Priority was given to contacts with the Balkans and this was reflected in icons and wall-paintings. Yet, on the whole, from this time we see the increasing dominance in Tver painting of the aesthetic and spiritual ideals common throughout Russia. Frescoes reveal echoes of the works of Muscovite artists, including those of Andrei Rublev. In fact, this homogeneity was characteristic of Russian art during its period of flourishing in the fifteenth century. It is important, however, to stress the role that Tver played — a role significant as that of Moscow — in evolving the traditions common to all Russia. The evidence for this lies not only in surviving Gorodnia frescoes but also in a range of icons of Tver provenance dating from the first half of the fifteenth century (Cat. Nos. 10—15, 23, 27—68).

The majority of the preparatory sketches discovered in the Gorodnia Church of the Nativity, executed for the most part in black and brown tempera, are of heads and half-length figures. The best drawings are reminiscent of modern quick sketches and are notable for their grace and purity of line.

The wall-paintings produce a most unusual impression by virtue of their peculiar combination of intimacy and small dimensions with the greatness of the spiritual world of the personages portrayed. Of the surviving fragments, the least damaged are the scenes from the life of St John the Baptist in the diaconicon. The building

was apparently damaged by fire time and again, as most of the paint took on a rusty brown tinge and the light blues have almost totally disappeared. *The Nativity of St John the Baptist* (ill. 23) suffered less in this respect and its colour scheme of tender pinkish browns, mauves and pale blues provides a good idea of the airy radiance of the original colouring and of the restrained gentle forms. The classical contours of the figures echo the works of Muscovite painters, in particular the circle of Andrei Rublev (frescoes in the Cathedral of the Dormition-on-the-Gorodok in Zvenigorod, *c.* 1400; frescoes in the Cathedral of the Dormition in Vladimir, 1408; icons executed in the first third of the fifteenth century). Another scene, depicting the angel leading the infant St John the Baptist into the desert, reveals a direct affinity with the Vladimir wall-paintings executed by Andrei Rublev and Daniil Chorny, particularly in the softness and inner light of the images. Yet the Gorodnia frescoes are characterized by greater intimacy, visible in the use of detail, and the sharpness of the drawing, which partly echo the world of early Tver painting, even though they are but a pale reflection of former ideals. The style of the Gorodnia wall-paintings serves as an indication of a breathtaking shift in the domain of the visual arts.

The decoration of the Gorodnia church, commissioned by the Prince of Tver and undertaken by the best painters, represents the dominant trend in early fifteenth-century Tver art and is important for the assessment of the standards of local icon-painting both at this time and later. Indeed, compared with the Gorodnia frescoes even the best of the later miniatures in the *Chronicle of Georgius Hamartolos* appear modest and unpretentious, if not truly provincial. Particularly striking, however, is the contrast between these frescoes and works such as the icon of the *Archangel Michael* (Cat. Nos. 8, 9).

Behind these contrasts probably lay a division within Tver art between what we might term court or metropolitan art and peripheral or provincial art, the latter term covering not only works executed outside Tver but even some produced within the city itself. Such works are not always linked with folk art, although a folkloric basis is not infrequent. Thus, fifteenth-century Tver painting clearly reflects the duality of medieval feudal culture; throughout this century until Tver's loss of independence these two trends co-existed and, whilst energetically interacting, did not fuse. Whereas the metropolitan trend was oriented towards the dominant artistic tendencies, changing as they changed, the provincial trend was more uniform and was primarily conservative in its outlook; the first trend shared an affinity with chiefly Muscovite and Balkan art, provincial works were not infrequently closer to Novgorod and Pskov icons.

Several icons characteristic of the metropolitan trend, their main stylistic features similar to those of the frescoes of the Gorodnia Church of the Nativity, may be dated to the first decades of the fifteenth century. The earliest is a half-length depiction of St Barbara and may be placed at the very start of the fifteenth century (Cat. Nos. 10, 11). Though its provenance has not been proven, the painting has parallels with later works whose Tver origin is supported by documents (Cat. Nos. 12—14). The light blue ground, perhaps the salient feature of the icon, clearly derives from wall-painting, as may the device of outlining the saint's figure in white. Contributing to the overall decorative impact are the contrasting yet harmonious combinations of the ground and the saint's attire, of her snowy white headgear and the glittering nimbus, whilst the wealth of gems and pearls imparts a festive appeal to the depiction of the saint in this icon.

The saint's austere, classically proportioned face betrays an introversion uncharacteristic of the icons of the artists of Rublev's circle. There seems to be no direct contact with the viewer. Yet the plasticity and the inner intensity of the image reveal a relationship with the forcefully depicted figures in the wall-paintings of the second half of the fourteenth century. But while the pronounced decorative quality and abundance of enlarged ornamental motifs can likewise be associated with earlier works (Cat. Nos. 1—5), the prevailing mood is one of tranquility and balance, demonstrating a leaning towards the new aesthetic and spiritual ideals. Perhaps as a result of Tver's contacts with Mount Athos, the artist was undoubtedly familiar with examples of Balkan painting of the turn of the fifteenth century, particularly their peculiar plastic illusionism, as in, for instance, such works of the so-called Moravian school as the frescoes of 1388/89 in the Church of St Andrew on the Traska River, or the frescoes of 1385—87 in the Ravenica Church in Serbia.

Similar stylistic echoes can be felt in the slightly later double-sided icon from the village of Vasilyevskoye near Staritsa (Cat. Nos. 12—14).

During the first decade of the fifteenth century the Cathedral of the Archangel Michael and the Church of St Nicholas in Staritsa, one of Tver principality's few large towns, were embellished with frescoes, apparently commissioned by the Prince of Tver. Though neither of the structures is extant, archaeologists have unearthed numerous fragments of stucco on their sites, as well as remnants of the lower tier of wall-paintings (a drapery or 'towel' frieze) that adorned the Cathedral of the Archangel Michael. These bear so-called epigraphic, or cryptographic, ornament imitating the lettering of an 'unknown' Oriental alphabet. Similar ornamentation can be encountered in both Novgorodian wall-paintings associated with the Balkan tradition and Muscovite icon-paintings of the turn of the fifteenth century. Subsequently it blended with Cyrillic lettering or generally relinquished all resemblance to any alphabet. During the fourteenth century it was especially popular in the Balkans, particularly in Greece, Serbia and Bulgaria, and the Staritsa frieze's rich profusion of calligraphic motifs reveals a familiarity with such Balkan models.

It is possible that, concurrently with the embellishment of the Staritsa churches, work was also undertaken in neighbouring princely estates (the village of Vasilyevskoye was later owned by the Mikulinsky princes, members of a junior branch of Tver royalty), and we may link with this the execution of a double-sided icon depicting the Virgin Hodegetria and St Nicholas — a choice of figures that was not unusual in processional icons of both Russian and Balkan provenance. Though the style of the two faces differs, this does not preclude both sides having been painted by one and the same artist. His obvious acquaintance with Balkan painting has given rise to the suggestion that he came either from Greece or Yugoslavia, but the entire character of the painting, the plastic treatment and the interpretation of the images — i.e. all the main elements — are in the mainstream of the Russian artistic tradition, and there is a manifest parallel with the peripheral trend in Tver art.

The colour scheme of the *Virgin Hodegetria* is based around the contrast between the light-coloured ground and the Virgin's mauvish-brown omophorion and the Infant Christ's reddish orange robe, heightened by sparse yet subtle means. The outline of the omophorion rather enriches than detracts from the plasticity, while the blue of the mobcap sets off the glitter of the gold surrounding the Virgin's face, emphasizing the symbolism of this device. Christ's chiton and himation are modelled by freely applied cinnabar tints in the folds and by thick golden hatching. For all the decorative approach to the modelling and the complex play of the fragmented folds, the plastic aspect of the figures is quite clear. The use of half-tones and additional hues in the garments is minimal, subordinated to the object of bringing out the faces — the conceptual and pictorial centre of the icon — heavily modelled faces that are traditional with regard to their colourful brilliance. The Virgin is both regal and benign, and she looks at the viewer with serene intensity. Meanwhile the Infant Christ's face seems tense, but he nevertheless radiates a mood of gentle restraint. The drawing is precise and summary, and the artist had a unified, spatial sense of form.

We see here an artistic approach new in terms of both orientation and standard, which would not appear to be associated with the preceding local tradition. On the whole, the *Hodegetria* may be related to that range of philosophical and aesthetic concepts which dominated Russian visual art at the time, and may thus be seen as a further milestone along the road already marked by the icon of *St Barbara* and the frescoes of the Gorodnia Church of the Nativity. Though in terms of its painting the *Hodegetria* is most closely related to the style of early fifteenth-century Muscovite icons, it has evident intonations of its own. In comparison with the radiant softness and ideal harmony of Muscovite icons on the same theme, the images on the Tver icon appear more vigorous, even though introverted, and there are some features which are reminiscent of earlier works such as the 'faceted' highlights on the Virgin's face and a certain expressiveness in the handling of the depiction of the Infant Christ and St Nicholas.

On the reverse, however, with its half-length depiction of St Nicholas, these reminiscences are even more distinct. The return to greater conventionality should

16. Helen, Mother of the Emperor Constantine the Great, Receiving Beggars and Monks in the Palace. Early 15th century. Illumination from the *Chronicle of Georgius Hamartolos*. Russian State Library, Moscow

be noted first of all. The purple cloak is modelled by means of several layers of white-lead brushstrokes, unlike the customary device employed in the early fifteenth century of tinting the reflections, and hence the muted tones of the highlights create the sensation of a flat plane. The folds are rigid and fragmented, the drawing only roughly relates to the form, while the rhythmical arrangement seems almost ornamental.

The head and the hand raised in benediction are, however, treated quite differently, with a greater sense of volume and a contrasting use of light and dark. Though the impression is one of an intense light source similar to that portrayed on the obverse, we have here a rich colour scheme with sharp transitions of colour from which softer half-tones have been excluded. The highlights are bright and varied with intricate contours which seem almost to form a pattern on the forehead and brows. The highlights in the locks of hair are particularly fanciful. The result of this stylization is the elimination of any sensation of mobility of form.

The treatment of the image of the saint should also be noted. Whereas the icon of St Barbara is marked by classical proportions and restrained power while the Virgin Hodegetria is benign and beautiful, the image of St Nicholas displays an ascetic intensity and profound introspection.

Earlier we had occasion to note the dual, changing nature of the works produced during the initial phase of Tver's artistic revival after its long period of stagnation. In the domain of painting the evolution of local traditions within the overall context of fifteenth-century culture is particularly pronounced. All works from this period, including the Royal Doors from Nektaryev (Cat. Nos. 25, 26) are unique and individual, each the product of creative experimentation and re-interpretation of a diverse range of sources.

As a result we see Tver producing in the mid-fifteenth century works that may be ranked without exaggeration among the best in Russian art, and the basis for this breathtaking upsurge was laid at the very start of the fifteenth century, a time of diverse cultural contacts and of vigorous artistic creativity.

A second processional icon from the village of Vasilyevskoye, with a patchily preserved scene of the Nativity of the Virgin (Cat. No. 15), marks the next step in

17. The Prophet Daniel. Early 15th century. Detail of the illumination *The Prophet Daniel Being Led Out of the Lions' Den* from the *Chronicle of Georgius Hamartolos*. Russian State Library, Moscow

23

the evolution of the dominant trend. Though we may, in principle, again associate it with the early fifteenth-century works of art to be found in Staritsa and its vicinity, its state of preservation precludes an exact dating, the more so as the surviving portions appear stylistically to be of a somewhat later date, and local features (partly akin to the *St Nicholas* on the reverse of the first Vasilyevskoye icon) are more pronounced. Yet, on the whole, there is a dominant sense of measured, attentuated rhythm. The icon is solemn yet intimate. The figures of the maidens bearing gifts and waving fans in front of the couch, upon which St Anne, the Virgin's mother, reclines, invoke distinct recollections of the finest examples of late fourteenth- and early fifteenth-century painting with their echoes of Muscovite icons and the Gorodnia frescoes. The girls' movements are flowing and their contours rounded. Meanwhile the treatment of the other figures, as seen in the fragments of St Anne and the serving woman in front of the basin, displays what we might construe as a departure from the period's prevalent aesthetic and a reversion to the earlier plastic structure. The drawing is simple, the lines emphatically straightened and, as before, the stylized forms are broken down into composite elements. The contour is rigid and vigorous. Highlighted planes serve to effect the modelling. Even so, the plentiful highlighting does not minimize the vibrancy of the colour scheme, based on a carefully balanced combination of light blues and purplish pinks, mauves, reds and brownish ochres. The artist has achieved that special softness and harmony which was characteristic of fifteenth-century painting and in this respect the icon seems closer to Muscovite art. The dominant graphic quality appears merely as a pale tribute to local tradition, while the dense grid of highlights and their vigorous drawing give the artist's style a certain degree of continuity with the early phase of local artistic evolution. The common Russian stylistical features of the period dominate.

18. Patericon of the Kiev Monastery of the Caves. 1406. Russian National Library, St Petersburg

The technique has been largely modified accordingly, as may be discerned in the figures of the maidens which are in a better state of preservation. There is less use of impasto and the contours of the forms have been empasized by a speedily applied,

19. Book of the Four Gospels. 1417. Museum of History, Architecture and Literature, Tver

soft brown outline, serving to accentuate their plasticity and elegance. The skilful calligraphic nature of the work is fully in accord with fifteenth-century tradition and we can see throughout the painter's love for refined beauty.

Linked to the same group are two icons from a half-length Deesis tier, namely the *Virgin* and *St John the Baptist* from the village of Obodovo near Torzhok (Cat. Nos. 16, 17; 18, 19) where they were probably produced. An object of perpetual strife, Torzhok belonged now to Novgorod, now to Tver. This was no major artistic centre; on the contrary, most of the building and painting seems to have been the work of master craftsmen from Novgorod. However, judging from these two icons, we have reason to assert that also active in Torzhok were master craftsmen from Tver, at least during the period when Torzhok's links with Novgorod were weaker, a time that coincided with Tver's cultural growth.

Though the painter who created the two icons remained within the bounds of the traditional iconographic canon, he was still able to leave the stamp of his own personality on both. In the *Virgin* his individualized approach is expressed in the left hand raised high in a gesture of prayer. As for the other icon, we should note the unusual three-quarter-face pose, the contrast in the folds of the garment and the rhythm of the outstretched hands. Yet the most important aspect of these icons is the sense of an unbroken link with the pictorial tradition of the first half of the fifteenth century. In place of that imperious impact upon the viewer so characteristic of earlier icons (Cat. Nos. 6, 7; 8, 9) or of the older icons of the dominant trend (such as the *St Nicholas* on the reverse of the icon from Vasilyevskoye), we now observe a soft, inspired radiance. Thus the Deesis composition, centred around the now lost figure of Christ, acquires new meaning, establishing a kinship with the Muscovite icons of Rublev's period. In these portayals of the Virgin and St John the Baptist interceding before the Saviour for the human race there is nothing of that heightened grief which often marked the more expressive and dynamic icons of the thirteenth and fourteenth centuries.

The reflection of contemporary artistic ideal is also conveyed through the icon's particular refinement. The softly blending half-tones and the pinks prevalent in the faces produce the impression of an inner glow, of ideal perfection. Yet at the

20. Church of the
Nativity of the Virgin in
the village of Gorodnia.
Ca. 1412. View from
southeast

same time the faces have a certain angularity and stylization of form which are clearly characteristic of local tradition, making the two icons from Obodovo good examples of the Tver version of the general Russian style, combining elements of both the dominant and the conservative trends.

Something similar is seen in the miniature icon of the *Nativity of the Virgin* (Cat. Nos. 20—22) from the Suzdal Convent of the Intercession of the Virgin, painted at the same time and now housed in the Russian Museum in St Petersburg.

In the fourteenth and fifteenth centuries Suzdal was a town of monasteries and convents which attracted donations from all major towns and regions of the Russian land. One particularly revered convent was that of the Intercession of the Virgin where many girls from the aristocracy, including those from princely families, took their vows. The gifts made to the convent were often notable for their artistic merits, and, besides many diverse items from Muscovy and Central Russia, they included works of Novgorod and Pskov provenance. It is possible that Tver feudal lords also contributed — something certainly supported by later documents; at any rate, the icon of the *Nativity of the Virgin* is unquestionably the work of a Tver painter of the first half of the fifteenth century.

Though very intimate in feel, this icon, which presents an abbreviated version of the episode, is nevertheless imposing in terms of composition. There are two scenes, one in which the handmaids greet St Anne, the other with the bathing of the Infant Mary. The simplicity and generalized nature of the lines — softly rounded and emphatically straight — create a sense of measured rhythm, while the precise architectural articulation and gradations of light and dark lend the icon spatial clarity. These qualities are further complemented by the even balance of the areas of colour, the confident combination of warm reds and a cold blue surrounded by different shades of yellowish and brownish ochre (the background was also ochre but was covered by repoussé work in silver during the sixteenth century). At the same time lines and the forms that they define are not without a certain acuteness and hidden dynamism. The fine linear hatching used to model the fabrics introduces a sense of fragmentation. The faces, painted with sharp contrasts of light and shadow, are tense and petrified. In the scene of the bathing of the Infant Virgin the figures are extremely expressive, particularly that of the serving woman holding the Child as she dips a hand into the basin to test the water.

This duality of style is not surprising in that it reflects the overall nature of Tver painting during the first half of the fifteenth century. We must mention that similar traits can be observed in the icons from Obodovo. But in the icons of the *Virgin* and *St John the Baptist* the forms are monumentalized, whereas in the *Nativity* they are markedly intimate.

Another icon, with a depiction of the Virgin Hodegetria and dating from the first half or middle of the fifteenth century, also betrays this duality of style and the courtly feel we saw in the *Nativity of the Virgin*. It was donated to the Trinity—St Sergius Monastery by the ruling family of a small duchy in the Tver principality, centred around Mikulin (Cat. No. 24).

As we noted earlier, the Mikulin princes were a junior branch of the Tver royal family. The inscription on the reverse of the icon bears the name of a Princess Anna, of which there were two — one at the turn of the fifteenth century, the other in the first half of the sixteenth century. Though it is hard to say which of the two is meant, the refined character of this small icon can clearly be explained by its association with this noble family.

Stylistically, the *Virgin Hodegetria* is markedly different from earlier pieces. The painter was obviously following a Moscow prototype, copying its iconography and draughtsmanship down to the minutest detail, as we can judge on the basis of several extant icons dating from the post-Rublevian period. Yet there is much here that sets the work apart from Moscow icons. The figures are heavy and impressive, the drawing complex and fragmented. Features such as the enamel-like surface, the thick paint layer, the precise definition of form and the static character of the rounded faces are more closely associated with archaic local fifteenth-century items. Despite the outward fidelity to the finest examples of contemporary Moscow painting, this Tver painter was of a more conservative bent.

Probably the most archaic and conservative works — in artistic terms — from the first half of the fifteenth century are the Royal Doors from the village of Nektaryev, near Tver (Cat. Nos. 25, 26). The stylized forms and the tense visages of St John Chrysostom and St Basil the Great relate more closely to earlier icons such as the fourteenth-century *Christ Pantocrator* (Cat. Nos. 6, 7) and the *Archangel Michael* of the turn of the fifteenth century (Cat. Nos. 8, 9). Like these works the Royal Doors produce an impression of something deeply provincial, which sets them apart from the above-mentioned group of icons from the first half of the fifteenth century. Their fundamental significance lies in the evidence they provide of the diverse nature of Tver icon-painting throughout this period, thus furnishing an explanation for the stylistic duality in some of the icons of the leading group, above all the *Nativity of the Virgin* and the *Virgin Hodegetria* (Trinity—St Sergius Monastery).

But at the same time the general Russian tendencies, even a direct address by local artists to Moscow painting, are indicative of the cardinal changes which had taken place in Tver's cultural development in the fifteenth century.

The history of the Tver principality during the first few decades of the fifteenth century is marked by major political achievements: for instance, in 1426 the Kashin appanage, whose rulers had constantly sought to ally themselves with Muscovy, was brought under control. Tver's consolidation coincided with a time of strife among its neighbours and as a result of internecine quarrels between the Moscow princes,

21. Church of the
Nativity of the Virgin
in the village of
Gorodnia. *Ca.* 1412. Apses

22. Church of the
Nativity of the Virgin
in the village of
Gorodnia. *Ca.* 1412.
Window in the south
wall

Tver again became a major feudal centre in the second quarter and middle of the fifteenth century, its cultural life flourishing once more.

It was apparently during this troubled period that some Muscovite craftsmen and artisans decided to move to more peaceful lands, including Tver, with its considerable number of building and painting projects. The direct involvement of Muscovite artists in these works is illustrated by, for instance, the impressively large icon of the *Metropolitan Peter* (Cat. No. 23) from the Deesis tier of Tver's largest and most esteemed monastery, the Otroch Monastery. Outwardly it compares with the best examples of post-Rublevian Moscow icons, having stylistic links with iconostases from Zvenigorod (*ca.* 1400) and from the Cathedral of the Dormition in Vladimir (shortly after 1408), both of which are attributed to Rublev himself. At any rate, in its spiritual perspicacity and the richness and harmony of its colour scheme the *Metropolitan Peter* is a truly striking example of local artistic creativity, and its painter may be ranked among the leading icon-painters in fifteenth-century Tver.

There is no question that masters of so high a standard could find employment in Tver. Unfortunately, chronicles furnish a far from full picture of construction in Tver at this period. More detailed information may be gleaned from the *Paean to the Pious Grand Prince Boris Alexandrovich*, ascribed to the monk Foma (usually held to be the sole author, although some scholars believe the manuscript to have been a collective effort). Probably written shortly after 1453, towards the close of the Prince's reign (1425—61), it includes much information on the construction projects undertaken by the Prince between the 1430s and the 1450s, describing the fortresses and churches (mostly of stone, but with some of wood) that were built in Tver, Kashin and smaller towns as extraordinarily grand with richly and artfully decorated interiors. The truth — or exaggeration — of these statements is hard to judge, as none of the buildings have survived. All that we have to go by are later, relatively undetailed, representations (ill. 1 and Cat. Nos. 181, 182).

Nevertheless, on the whole the scale of construction that the *Paean* describes seems more or less to reflect reality.

Coupled with the *Chronicle of the Tver Princes*, also dating from the mid-fifteenth century, the *Paean* furnishes a crucial source for studying the period, as it provides much factual evidence and illustrates the ideals and attitudes of local feudal society. Extolling the greatness of the Prince, its text has a clear social and political programme, emphasizing that if Constantinople (or Tsargrad) was the 'Second Rome', Tver was the 'New Rome', its prince the 'Second Constantine the Great' (the Emperor of Byzantium, 324—337) and the Principality of Tver was the sole worthy successor to the marvels of Byzantium and its role in world history.

Obviously this idealistic viewpoint could be adopted only after the capture of Constantinople by the Turks in 1453, a point Academician Nikolai Likhachev made when he published the *Paean* in 1908, and it is also explained by Tver's relative political stability and consequent flourishing cultural life.

As previously mentioned, fourteenth- and early fifteenth-century Tver writers tended to idealize contacts with Constantinople, and thus the *Paean* represents a natural development of this tendency. Yet the picture of the world fame and brilliance of Tver and its 'Caesar', Prince Boris Alexandrovich, is, of course, far-fetched. Time and again the text refers to the extensive fame of the prince "from the East unto the West and unto the very imperial city itself, that is, unto Rome itself". Here too we find wordy sermons supposedly delivered in praise of the Prince by churchmen all over the Orthodox world. It is suggested that such "praise... was heard by Foma, Tver's ambassador" at the Ecumenical Council in Ferrara and Florence. He indeed attended its sessions, which ended in 1439 by proclaiming the union of Western and Eastern Churches, an event greatly frowned upon in Russia. However, the reference to an eyewitness is in this case no more than a literary device. The contents of the 'speeches' are sheer fantasy, pure courtly rhetoric, as too are the extensive parallels drawn between the activities of the Prince of Tver and those of biblical heroes and the emperors of Byzantium and Rome. Only the final chapter, which is based on the chronicles, offers a relatively realistic picture of the situation during the reign of Boris Alexandrovich.

The 1450s, during which the *Paean* was produced, were actually a time when Muscovy's fortunes were very much on the rise after the end of internecine strife. In this situation contemporaries around the Prince of Tver could not but realize the brevity of the principality's flourishing. All the more striking therefore is the extraordinarily talented rhetoric of its author (or authors), which is so complex in form and abounds in literary associations.

Though the *Paean* stands alone in fifteenth-century Russian literature, many of the ideas it propounded were extensively elaborated upon later. Particularly popular was the idea of a 'new', Russian, Rome that lay at the basis of the sixteenth-century concept of state in which the role of the 'Third Rome' was naturally allotted to Moscow.

Generally speaking, Tver's cultural flourishing in the mid-fifteenth century was of profound significance for the whole of Russia.

We should note that the dominant atmosphere of this period was responsible for the views espoused by the Tver merchant Afanasy Nikitin, the first Russian to reach distant India, whose travel notes comprise his celebrated *Journey Beyond the Three Seas* (1466—72 or 1468—75). In this work of a truly national character Russia appears as a single whole. "There is no land in the world like it... May the Russian land be well ordered and may there be justice there," Nikitin wrote... In addition, the *Journey* furnishes a vivid picture of Tver's urban culture. Indeed, this work is remarkable for its author's profound interest in his surroundings, for his unprejudiced attitude to their diversity and to the customs of the different countries he visited, and for its precise, descriptive language which borders on the colloquial.

Unfortunately, many essential details of cultural life in Tver in the mid-fifteenth century are still unknown to us, in particular we can only conjecture as to the scale of literary activity and the copying of books. On the other hand, it is obvious that the level of erudition in Tver society was high; moreover, we know that the monastery libraries in Tver were very rich and even the Metropolitan Photius (1408/10—1431) often consulted them.

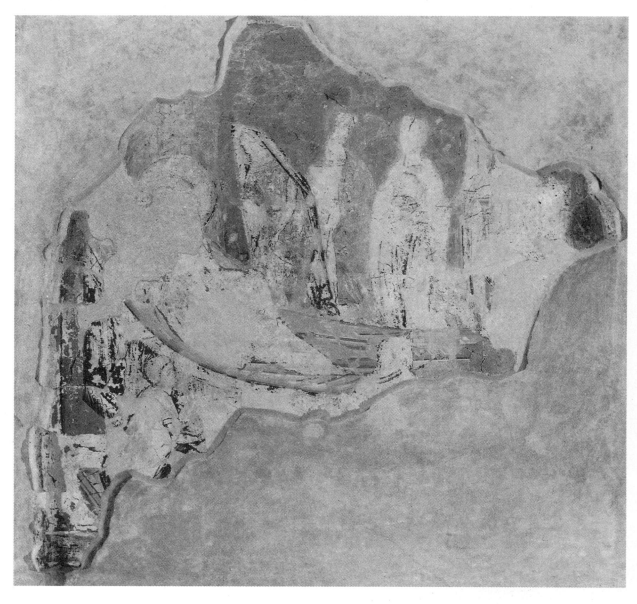

23. Nativity of St John the Baptist. First quarter of the 15th century. Detail of wall-painting from the diaconicon of the Church of the Nativity of the Virgin in the village of Gorodnia. Tver Picture Gallery

24. Half-length figure of the Virgin. First quarter of the 15th century. Drawing in black tempera on a pillar in the church in the village of Gorodnia

25. St John the Baptist in the Wilderness. First quarter of the 15th century. Detail of wall-painting from the diaconicon of the church in the village of Gorodnia. Tver Picture Gallery

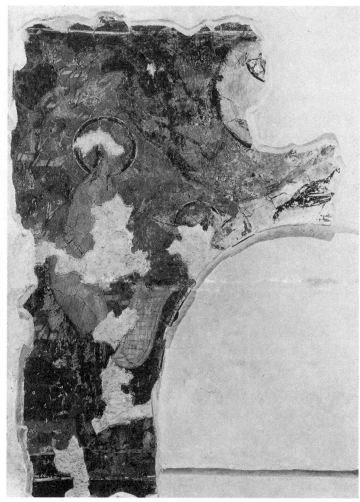

Prince Boris Alexandrovich is also mentioned in one of the oldest surviving Russian manuscripts, the late eleventh-century copy of the *Sinai Patericon*, now in the Historical Museum in Moscow. It bears traces of restoration carried out in the fourteenth and fifteenth centuries. The Prince's name figures here alongside several comments and three pen-and-ink drawings (ills. 26, 27). Two of these drawings, which are small pieces done in the margins, are clearly reminiscent of the sketches made for the wall-paintings in the Gorodnia Church of the Nativity. The third full-page drawing, of an apostle or prophet, is a splendid example of graphic art in the first half of the fifteenth century. Despite its poor state of preservation, its virtuoso execution and plastic quality are obvious. All this indicates a continual interest in this ancient manuscript, on the part of local artists among others.

Apart from this manuscript, the *Paean* and several tales and excerpts from annals and chronicles, a clear idea of the breadth of cultural and literary interest in Tver during the period in question is provided by a codex from the Rogozhskoye cemetery collection. The only illustrated work in this codex, the *Journey of the Archimandrite Agrephenius*, describes a pilgrimage to the Holy Land, most probably undertaken by this Father Superior of one of Tver's monasteries in the 1370s. Much space in this work is allotted to a description of the architecture and interior decoration of buildings in Jerusalem, the most famous and important of which are reproduced as pen-and-ink sketches in the text (ill. 28). This manuscript, of which only two copies are known, is the oldest Russian illustrated guide, a genre extremely popular in its day.

Very little has survived of Tver's unquestionably rich legacy of jewellery and applied arts from the first half and middle of the fifteenth century. The most remarkable item of the period is a boar-spear which belonged to the Grand Prince Boris Alexandrovich and, together with many of medieval Tver's relics, eventually found its way into the treasury of the Grand Prince of Moscow and can now be seen in the Kremlin Armoury. The piece displays a complex décor technique. Engraved silver plaques embellishing the shank present eight allegorical scenes of a diverse nature which make it clear that this was a ceremonial weapon intended to reinforce the prestige of its owner. Thus, the scenes depict the Prince's law-making activities as well as his justice and valour — the same complex of ideas we find in the *Paean*.

It was during the second quarter or middle of the fifteenth century that a group of icons of the Deesis, Church Feasts and Prophets tiers (Cat. Nos. 27—68), which may justly be regarded as the zenith of Tver painting, was created. There are still some blank spots in the history of these icons. In 1626 they were in the Tver Cathedral of the Transfiguration but were clearly unsuited to this location, as they were larger than befitted the dimensions of this old, late thirteenth-century edifice. The conflagration that swept through the cathedral in 1537 supports the opinion that these icons were installed later than that date and presumably were transferred from one or other of the big Tver churches erected in the reign of Boris Alexandrovich, most probably the Cathedral of SS Boris and Gleb and/or the Cathedral of the Archangel Michael. Most of these icons were discovered in Kashin and thus scholars have come to term them the Kashin range.

Of course not all the icons from the three tiers have survived. Some disappeared early, as can be gleaned from the 1626 register of the Cathedral of the Transfiguration, others later, when they were already in Kashin. On some the initial paint layer has been almost completely lost, particularly on the icons of the Deesis (Cat. Nos. 27—37) and Prophets (Cat. Nos. 63—68) tiers and also on the *Entry into Jerusalem* from the Church Feasts tier (Cat. Nos. 53—55).

The salient feature of most of these icons is their orientation towards the Paleologue style and, partly, also towards the early fifteenth-century Muscovite style of painting. This can be clearly seen in both iconography and the manner of execution. The works represent an organic fusion of national features with elements drawn from Balkan painting — the spatial arrangement and some of the techniques employed.

This is especially true of the Church Feasts icons. In all likelihood the prevalent mood during Tver's short-lived heyday gave the brilliance and grandeur of Byzantium a particular appeal in the eyes of the prince's court. The art of Constantinople was seen as the sole worthwhile criterion — which was logical in the context of intellectual and spiritual life in Tver at the time, even though this fascination with the Byzantine ideal would appear at first sight to conflict with the dominant trends in the evolution of Russian art.

We have already had occasion to note the diverse influences which mark the history of Tver art in one period or another. The period of Tver's flourishing saw a particularly large number of contacts. The different Byzantinisms infiltrating the local cultural scene often had an 'anti-Muscovite' side to them, a phenomenon which continued into the middle of the fifteenth century, with the rivalry acquiring a more abstract form only outwardly. Consonant with the thesis of Tver's 'elect' status was the metropolitan character of its painting, a metropolitanism which the princely court of Tver continued to associate with Constantinople, not with neighbouring Muscovy.

The works under discussion reveal a fundamentally different level of approach to the Byzantine, or rather the Balkan tradition as a whole. We do not observe here any direct imitation of concrete prototypes. The manner of execution suggests that the painters had a broad knowledge of different artistic tendencies of the fourteeenth and fifteenth centuries, which they endeavoured to creatively re-interpret. Their efforts influenced subsequent development. A similar synthetizing attitude to the Balkan heritage is characteristic of Muscovite painting of the turn of the sixteenth century and later. A good example of this is the work of Dionysius, the most eminent of painters after Rublev. Thus, a kind of conservatism went hand in hand with an innovative resolution of the tasks which Tver artists set themselves.

Though the icons in question would not appear to have any direct similarity with earlier local works, with the exception of the icon of the *Metropolitan Peter*, the

26. Figure of an Apostle (?). *Ca.* mid-15th century. Pen-and-ink drawing from the Sinai Patericon. 11th century. Historical Museum, Moscow

aesthetic aims and style coincide with the character and prevalent trends of fifteenth-century Tver culture.

The senior among the three or four painters, who worked on this group of icons, was responsible for the central icon of the Deesis tier and for most of the icons in the Church Feasts and Prophets tiers. Nothing akin to his efforts in scale can be found in all of preceding Tver painting, to say nothing of the extensive artistic erudition, temperament and virtuoso craftsmanship.

The images of Christ in Majesty (Cat. Nos. 27—33) and of the Prophets (Cat. Nos. 65—68) are truly majestic and of an intellectual refinement. The colour scheme of the Deesis and Prophets icons is built on a combination of light and dark blues, browns, scarlets and greens, with an intricate play of nuances which attenuates the contrasts. The forms are large and simple. The manner of the best and leading artist of the group is remarkable for its inspired nature, subtle wealth of technique and free-flowing, almost sketchy character. The light tone of the field creates a sense of spatial depth. Three Church Feasts icons, the *Nativity of Christ*, the *Presentation in the Temple* and the *Raising of Lazarus*, are in a good state of preservation, and fully illustrate the creative individuality and virtuoso skill of this artist and his perspicacious characterizations.

The painter who produced the *Baptism of Christ* (Cat. Nos. 56, 57) was most probably an apprentice of the leading artist, as he has clearly imitated his master's manner, achieving a similar lyrical expressiveness in his work. Although the softness and spiritual refinement of his figures bears an affinity to the *Nativity of Christ* and the *Presentation in the Temple*, his manner is less confident and deft, while his interpretation is not as expressive. The icon of the *Ascension* (Cat. Nos. 58—60) would appear to be further apart and more independent, yet its execution too manifestly reveals an attempt to follow in the footsteps of the master painter. Its author may have also produced the *Descent of the Holy Ghost* (Cat. Nos. 61, 62), which likewise displays differences from the works of the leading painter.

We are unable to say exactly how many painters were involved in creating the icons, as many of the surviving pieces are in no good state of preservation. However, it is quite clear that the chief's manner was emulated by the others in the team. The stylistic integrity of his works is an indication of the extremely conducive conditions in which the master was able to develop his artistic individuality, conditions that Tver was never to experience again. Without exaggeration, we may describe the works created by him and under his supervision as the high point of local art.

As we noted earlier, at every stage of evolution Tver painting retained its diversity and stylistic heterogeneity. Alongside great refinement we find pieces that are profoundly archaic and provincial in their conception and style. This latter category includes a Deesis tier and the doors displaying the figures of archangels, that lead to the prothesis and the diaconicon (Cat. Nos. 69—86). These works entered the Tretyakov Gallery in Moscow from the collection of the art historian Alexander Anisimov; their possible original location may have been the Church of the Nativity of the Holy Virgin in the Coachmen's (Yamskaya) quarter in Tver.

These works represent an elaboration on the style of Tver's early painting, a style that is patently conservative and provincial for the second half of the fifteenth century when they were most produced. However, the impact of prevailing trends can be observed in the superficial modification of this style, which is expressed primarily in the softer handling of the central images (*Christ in Majesty*, the *Virgin* and also the *Archangel Michael* on the doors leading into the diaconicon). On the whole, though, their artistic structure displays a superabundance of forms that serves to generate a sense of static yet heightened expressiveness. The somewhat overdone stress on inner tension in the icon of *St Gregory the Divine* links these figures with the images of earlier times. In other words, we find archaic Tver painting persisting here.

The pronounced leaning towards painting of the turn of the fifteenth century, the smoothness of manner, the polished character of the techniques and approaches employed, indeed, the near automatic execution have parallels in the paintings created in other artistic centres, particularly Novgorod. We may deduce therefore that with regard to conservative works Tver was also in the mainstream of the processes occurring in fifteenth-century art. However, its innovations produced contradictory results. The erstwhile impulsiveness had now yielded on the whole to a greater degree of restraint. The crucial artistic elements are now largely expressed only superficially.

A greater degree of artistic integrity in the fusion of the conservative approach with the style of the epoch can be found in the *Entry into Jerusalem*, an icon from the Church of the Intercession of the Holy Virgin in Moscow's Rogozhskoye Cemetery (Cat. Nos. 89, 90). The fact that this icon belonged to a congregation of the Old Believers virtually excludes the possibility of clarifying its history, since the creation of such collections cannot be traced. However, this work's affinity with such icons as the *Mikulinsky Virgin Hodegetria* (Cat. No. 24) and the *Nativity of the Virgin* from the Suzdal Cathedral of the Intercession (Cat. Nos. 20—22) seems to be quite obvious. Indeed the enamel-like, vivid impasto, even though heightened with white, a colour scheme based on cold tones, and the heavy proportions and sharply etched forms are all elements that echo to some extent the characteristics of the Deesis icons from Alexander Anisimov's collection bearing the enduring features of fifteenth-century Tver icon-painting.

Though the creative style of the artist would appear to be unquestionably linked with Tver's cultural heyday, the *Entry into Jerusalem* seems to have been executed after the mid-fifteenth century. Instead of generalization we find here an emphasis on detail and the scene bears an almost ceremonial character. The festive nature of the welcome, the delight of those greeting Christ is stressed by the portrayal of children, particularly the group engaged in extracting a splinter from a foot; in fact this subject is rarely found in Russian painting and indicates the artist's familiarity with the iconography of Balkan art.

The artist who painted the icon of *St Nicholas with Christ and the Virgin* (Cat. Nos. 87, 88) — probably executed around the middle of the fifteenth century or a little later — also reveals a familiarity with Muscovite tradition as well as with the techniques of the painters who created the iconostases of the Cathedral of the Transfiguration or the Kashin church. The icon also shares an affinity to the *Metropolitan Peter* from the Otroch Monastery (Cat. No. 23). The medallion-enclosed image is similar in type to the Mikulinsky *Virgin Hodegetria*, its half-length figure is marked by the same restrained expressiveness, while the Virgin's headdress, the omophorion, is decorated with large gold hatching. The gentle nobility of the appearance of Christ and of the central half-length figure are related to the Muscovite artistic and spiritual ideal. The icon of *St Nicholas with Christ and the Virgin*, however, differs from the contemporary Muscovite icons in the much lighter, semi-translucent modelling. The modelling of the face and hands with their graduated glazed highlights, the barely suggested locks of hair and the free-flowing drawing are particularly expressive. It is this drawing that brings to mind the techniques employed by the artists who painted the tiers for the Tver Cathedral. The icon is remarkable for its harmony between image and form, in which respect it reveals a sense of fidelity to the art of Andrei Rublev and his followers. Thus, the style of this work confirms an earlier hypothesis as to the broad and varied contacts that Tver icon-painters maintained with their counterparts of Muscovy.

Indeed, had there been no such links we would be hard put to explain how Tver produced an icon like the *Synaxis of the Virgin* (Cat. Nos. 91—94), though we must say that its relationship with the Tver tradition of the second half of the fifteenth century is hypothetical. However, the rather cold colours of this piece with its wealth of tints, painterly complexity and somewhat rigid plastic structure, which may be deduced only from the surviving fragments, and its element of expressiveness accord with the traditions of fifteenth-century Tver icon-painting. The solemn spatial character of this composition on the theme of a Christmas canticle displays an affinity

with the icons from the Church Feasts tier of the Cathedral of the Transfiguration (Cat. Nos. 38—43; 44—48); the manner of execution is equally temperamental, free-flowing and effectively picturesque.

Only the subject could be considered unexpected in Tver icon-painting, as the Mariological theme was more popular with Muscovite artists, particularly in the final decads of the fifteenth century. However, the style precludes any direct link with Muscovite art and suggests that a late fifteenth-century date is hardly likely. The composition derives directly from works produced in the Balkans where the subject was a common one in the fourteenth century. It is Balkan prototypes which lie behind the treatment of the 'heavenly firmament' in a way rarely seen in Russian art, that is, in the shape of a broad arc with angels. This detail is more typical of the Southern Slavonic and Byzantine icons of the fifteenth century. Given Tver's active contacts with the Balkans in the fourteenth and first half of the fifteenth century, its artists' familiarity with such a rare intricate iconography appears logical. However, we would think more probable that this is a case of the influences of Muscovite icon-painting, which were pronounced in Tver in the second half of the fifteenth century.

The Deesis tier icons of the *Virgin* and *St John the Baptist* (Cat. Nos. 95, 96; 97—100), like the icon of *St Barbara* (Cat. Nos. 10, 11), are of Uglich provenance. Both relate to the problem of the creative legacy of the artists who painted the ensemble from the Tver Cathedral along with this ensemble's subsequent interpretation. Though these two icons were clearly painted later, they are so closely related to the Tver Cathedral group of the second quarter or middle of the fifteenth century, that it would be only logical to conclude that they are the handiwork of either the chief artist who worked on the iconostasis or his pupil. The similarity is particularly strong in the draughtsmanship, the colour scheme and the method of glazing. Yet, there is much here that looks different. The forms are more stylized and fragile, a mood of intimacy has superseded the former imposing monumentality, the representations, especially that of St John, are more angular and the manner of execution would seem to display a deliberate virtuoso affectation. The style no longer has any concrete relationship to Tver painting; rather it is representative of the artistic culture of Russia generally. Indeed, the refined artistry is comparable only with

27. Head of a *starets*. Mid-15th century. Pen-and ink drawing from the Sinai Patericon. 11th century. Historical Museum, Moscow

28. Illustration to the *Journey of the Archimandrite Agrephenius*. From the Rogozhsky Codex. Mid-15th century. Russian State Library. Moscow

29. The Evangelist
Matthew. Illumination
from the *Book of the
Four Gospels*. 1478.
Museum of Tatarstan,
Kazan

30. St John the Divine
and Prochorus. Illumina-
tion from the *Book of the
Four Gospels*. 1478.
Museum of Tatarstan,
Kazan

the works of the best Muscovite painters of the second half and close of the fifteenth century, especially Dionysius, whose earlier icons of the 1480s reveal an awareness of the experience of the artists of the Kashin circle or painters of a kindred spirit.

Thus the *Old Testament Trinity* (1484—85) from the local icons tier of the iconostasis of the Cathedral of the Dormition in the Monastery of St Joseph of Volokolamsk (Cat. Nos. 101—103) is proof that Dionysius, Moscow's leading icon-painter, maintained direct contacts with artists of Tver origins who shared his artistic concept. The archives of this monastery inform us that the icon, probably produced for the Cathedral's consecration in 1485, was the work of the *starets* Paisii. This icon is the only one that has survived from the artist's entire working career which we can trace up to the early sixteenth century, although church records tell us of many more.

Since in its execution this icon clearly calls to mind the icons of the Cathedral of the Transfiguration, we can assume that Paisii either had links with its team of painters, or perhaps was even one of them — not the leader though.

At the same time the style of the *Old Testament Trinity* indicates a mastery of Muscovite tradition, as is shown by the gentler rhythm and the consummate grandeur of the figures. The faces have been extremely finely glazed. The prevailing atmosphere in art at the time was one of idealization of Rublev's work (the iconography of the *Old Testament Trinity* derives from his celebrated icon) and of veneration of the talent of Dionysius, and this could not but have influenced Paisii; hence his icon may equally be regarded as being already in the mainstream of the Muscovite school of painting.

Paisii was not the only artist of Tver origin to have taken up residence at the Monastery of St Joseph of Volokolamsk. His colleagues both at the close of the fifteenth century and later included scribes from Tver, Kashin and Mikulin. To understand why they had settled there, we must necessarily address ourselves to the political and cultural background of Tver at this time.

In the years after 1461, when Mikhail, son of Boris Alexandrovich, was enthroned as the Grand Prince of Tver, the principality's activity gradually declined.

31. The Transfiguration.
Illumination from a
Hymn Book. Turn of the
16th century. Tver Archives

The Grand Prince of Moscow fully and decisively established himself as head of the Russian state. In 1485 the Principality of Tver was annexed, forcing Mikhail to flee, first to Lithuania and subsequently to Poland. Ivan III of Moscow entered Tver entrusting reins of government there to his son. Since even after 1485 Tver remained a potential danger to the authority of the Grand Prince of Moscow, many of its treasures, archives and holy relics were transferred to Moscow, whose cultural influence thus grew. One energetic proponent of Moscow's policies and aesthetics was Bishop Vassian (1477—1507), of the Strigin-Obolensky family, a close associate of Joseph Volotsky. As early as 1478, he commissioned an illuminated *Book of the Four Gospels*, a copy of a Muscovite manuscript apparently from the Grand Prince's scriptorium; in the sixteenth century the Tver codex found its way to Kazan. Most of the illuminations bear a close resemblance to the contemporary Muscovite miniatures of the 1470s and 1480s (ill. 30). However, the first miniature which portrays St Matthew (ill. 29) is the handiwork of a painter of the conservative trend. The leaning towards the archaic tradition in this miniature is obviously determined by the worldview of the artist who defiantly opposed the artistic innovations of Boris Alexandrovich.

Apparently the cultural upswing of the mid-fifteenth century in Tver affected only a relatively small class of its society, namely the prince's court; hence when the situation changed in 1485, conservative trends again came into prominence, most probably due to the greater activity at the turn of the sixteenth century of local craftsmen and artisans. In the final analysis it is their creative endeavour that is to be credited for Tver having preserved its artistic autonomy right up to the mid-sixteenth century, although painting in other Volga towns, such as Yaroslavl, Nizhny Novgorod and even such an old independent centre as Rostov, was already evolving within the mainstream of the Muscovite tradition as the sixteenth century began.

The same circle of artists which produced the miniature of *St Matthew* was responsible for the leaf from a set of Royal Doors which, it has been suggested, came from the Church of the Nativity in Tver's Yamskaya quarter; a Royal Doors scene depicting *St Matthew and Sancta Sophia the Holy Wisdom*; and an icon of *St John the Divine* of unknown provenance (Cat. Nos. 104; 105; 113). Each of the three illustrates distinctive facets of Tver painting in the second half of the fifteenth century. Though the artists who painted these pieces were not isolated from the dominant, primarily Muscovite, trend determining the style of the epoch, we perceive these, however, through the prism of a particular local artistic awareness, that calls to mind the laconic and precise forms of contemporary Novgorodian icon-painting. Yet the basic impression is produced by the integrity of the image and the underlying tradition, by a method of working which although simplified is nevertheless of high artistic merit, as is illustrated by the subtle colour combinations of the Royal Doors leaf, the resonant colour scheme and plasticity of the scene portraying St Matthew and the intricate forms imparted to the half-length figure of St John.

The iconography of these pieces, especially the representation of Sancta Sophia the Holy Wisdom as the source of inspiration for the Evangelists, demonstrates a continued interest in the art of the Balkans. It is as if the painters of this circle undertook to carry forward into the new era local artistic trends of the turn of the fifteenth century, and although they were familiar with subsequent works of the leading tendency they had not lost a democratic edge in their creative efforts.

The fact that artists active in Tver at the close of the fifteenth century were aware of a considerable range of artistic phenomena is also confirmed by a group of works that may provisionally be termed Byzantinesque. These are the *Dormition* (Cat. Nos. 106—112) and two icons from a half-length Deesis tier, namely *Christ Pantocrator* and the *Apostle Paul* (Cat. Nos. 114—116; 117, 118).

Experts regard the *Dormition* as a brilliant interpretation of late Paleologue style. In this icon, the so-called 'cloud' iconographic scheme depicting the apostles miraculously wafted towards the couch upon which the Virgin lies, a theme that acquired popularity from the second half of the fifteenth century, has assumed a consummate classical perfection. An organic reflection of Paleologue prototypes is combined with an affinity to works echoing the local conservative tendency. In this sense we may view the icon of the *Entry into Jerusalem* (Cat. Nos. 89, 90) and the scene from the Royal Doors (Cat. No. 104) as the closest parallels to the *Dormition*. The Byzantinesque elements set the icon apart from the leading trends in Russian painting of the period, while demonstrating nevertheless an unbroken line of continuity with all Tver's preceding artistic evolution. This paradox holds true in principle for all Tver culture in the twilight of the city's independence. Present at the same time is a high degree of artistry deriving from Tver's still recent upward swing. The structure and draughtsmanship of the *Dormition* are precise and exact, while its forms are extremely plastic. The scene is permeated by a pale blue light enveloping the intensively radiant scarlet covering of the Virgin's couch. The prevalence of cold tints stresses the restrained yet dramatic action and the reserved expressiveness of the images portrayed.

The fact that the icon was discovered in Minsk would appear to support the hypothesis that it was commissioned by Prince Mikhail Borisovich of Tver after he fled to Lithuania. There is some amount of indirect evidence indicating that the Prince, who died around 1505, maintained his own court in Minsk. There is information about his connections with the Radziwills; according to one story his daughter was married to one of the members of this princely family, who owned estates in the neighbourhood of Minsk. The family gallery in the Nieswiez Castle possessed a portrait of Mikhail, of Polish workmanship and painted at the close of the sixteenth century or at the beginning of the seventeenth (now in the Art Museum of Minsk).

Another aspect of the same artistic tendency is found in the Deesis tier icons of *Christ Pantocrator* and *Apostle Paul* (Cat. Nos. 114—116; 117, 118). The central *Christ Pantocrator* icon is undeniably similar to Late Paleologue painting; its refined iconography blends a sense of illusion with the stylized smoothness of volumes. Its shining cold forms and sombre colour scheme accord with the passionless image that seems isolated from the viewer. The second icon is painted in a simpler and more spontaneous manner; it has more of the customary expressiveness and sharp graphic accents imparting to this half-length figure of the Apostle an individuality and philosophical significance, even though the Byzantine prototype is also obvious in this expressive depiction.

Though Tver continued to maintain ties with the Patriarchy even after the fall of Constantinople, we have no information available that would attest to visits to Mount Athos by people from Tver during the second half or end of the fifteenth century. However, early on in the sixteenth century Tver did despatch embassies there bearing gifts. Local society continued throughout this century to evince interest in Greek culture; no wonder the translator and writer Maxim the Greek who was exiled to Tver in 1531 found a favourable audience there and was able to teach his native tongue. It is possible that Tver painters were familiar with examples of post-Byzantine painting — from the period following the fall of Constantinople in 1453. Still, the resemblance that these two icons, especially that of *Christ Pantocrator*, bear to such art, may be purely superficial in character. Their style may possibly derive from earlier Balkan works, with which Tver painters were very familiar. More important and more to the point here is the position from which they were interpreted locally in the late fifteenth century.

During the second half and end of this century, when Tver's cultural life gradually declined, recollections of past, still recent, brilliance, and concomitant nostalgic tendencies, must have dominated, above all, in the upper classes. In defiance of Moscow's mounting cultural and artistic impact, Tver turned to the art of the Balkan world, seeing it as a firm standard that would be its salvation. Consequently the icon of *Christ Pantocrator* may be viewed as one of the last specimens of courtly paintings. The trend which it represents failed to advance further and remained isolated in the world of Russian painting.

The lot of Tver's finest artists of the late fifteenth century is indicative. The painter who created the *Dormition* most likely settled in Lithuania, while the two others who painted the *Christ Pantocrator* and the *Apostle Paul* were working on the principality's northern periphery. This is evidence of the migration of Tver's artisans, mostly to Moscow in the hope of receiving steady, large commissions.

As we have mentioned earlier, the Monastery of St Joseph of Volokolamsk was one of the centres where artisans and craftsmen from Tver actively collaborated with representatives of contemporary Muscovite culture. One possible result of this cooperation is the manuscript of a hymn book from the turn of the sixteenth century. Some of the illuminations are by top Moscow painters, but some are patently the work of Tver artists with archaic leanings (ill. 31). At the close of the fifteenth century and later Tver scribes displayed a high standard and produced a large volume of work, which is why it was quite logical to rely on the services of the Tver-born copyists active at the Monastery of St Joseph of Volokolamsk. Unlike the miniatures the ornamental decoration of the local manuscripts reveals a greater preference for all-Russian pro-Muscovite designs and motifs — which is well illustrated by the embellishment of codices produced in Tver itself that are found in the library of the Monastery of St Joseph of Volokolamsk. The headpieces of the *Annotated Gospel* that was written at the Zheltikov Monastery in 1530 (ill. 33) show the enduring Balkan plaited ornamentation and are virtually undistinguishable from the decoration done in the capital itself.

It was not only in Tver itself that life changed when the principality was annexed by Muscovy in 1485. Muscovite liegemen gradually settled in the territories around Tver with only a few minor princely appanages retaining some semblance of independence. The local forces of opposition were finally demolished when Ivan the Terrible's *oprichniks* ravaged Tver in 1570.

Prior to that massacre Tver had remained a major trading and artisan centre, especially famous for its master masons who travelled and worked far from the city. We know, for instance, of buildings erected in Novgorod's Khutyn Monastery in 1536—37, in the Svensk Monastery outside Briansk in 1567 and in Volokolamsk

itself in 1541, where by that time the work of Tver masons had already become traditional. Though the work of the masons from Tver has been but little studied thus far, the uniqueness of the structures they erected is self-evident. Two good examples are the so-called Church of the White Trinity built in Tver itself in 1563—64 (ill. 32) and the Cathedral of the Orsha Monastery outside Tver, which is of austere appearance, has only simple architectural embellishment and was probably built shortly before 1567. In Tver itself and in the lands of the former Tver principality new building was commissioned chiefly by the local merchant classes and the monasteries.

In Staritsa, Kashin and especially in neighbouring Kaliazin, many Moscow-trained masons and artists were active, and this markedly influenced the work of their local colleagues — indeed some of the icons from Kashin and Kaliazin which these created are already accepted as Muscovite handiwork.

In Tver itself painting evolved along a different line. The sixteenth century here too spelled the logical retreat on all fronts of the local inherited stylistic features, yielding to common Russian artistic standards and a distinct decline to a certain provincial level. But such an assessment is correct only if we consider the period in question as a whole.

The work of painters active in the first half and middle of the sixteenth century displays a complex blend of Tver tradition, marked by obvious preferences for earlier prototypes, with distinct influences from the dominant, Muscovite, artistic trends. A case in point is the icon of the *Old Testament Trinity* (Cat. Nos. 119, 120), whose state of preservation is patchy at best, and which carries a later inscription, patently erroneous, giving its date of painting as 1561. This fine piece, charged with tints of a refined intensity, shows primarily a tendency towards the simultaneous expression of pomp and intimacy that was characteristic of the style of the early sixteenth century. Though the link with local tradition would appear veiled and secondary, it is patently re-introduced in the scene at the bottom of the icon, which depicts the killing of the calf. A changed manner and fragmentary, expressive forms, however, cause us to recall much earlier works such as the Suzdal icon of the *Nativity of the Virgin* (Cat. Nos. 20—22).

A similar duality is typical of a relief-carved icon of the *Virgin Hodegetria* from the Monastery of St Nicholas of the Kamelaukion near Kashin (Cat. No. 121) and a richly mounted small painted icon on the same theme (Cat. No. 122). While the former combines the characteristic Tver stylization of ponderous forms with a filigree embellishment, which is peculiar to monuments of the first third of the sixteenth century, the latter is extremely sumptuous and though much here is reminiscent of the *Mikulinsky Virgin Hodegetria*, it can no longer be separated from the general Russian, basically pro-Muscovite, tradition of the period... All that the Tver artist has introduced is an element of heightened expressiveness which imparts a certain suggestion of Mannerism. It is possible that this icon too was donated to the Trinity-St Sergius Monastery by a member of the Tver aristocracy.

Among the most remarkable works created by local painters in the first third of the sixteenth century are three Deesis tier icons of monumental form from the Church of the Dormition in Tver (Cat. Nos. 123—128). In the central *Christ in Majesty* the interpretation of Christ as a stern judge is stressed by the expressive draughtsmanship and the contrasting colours. The paintwork as a whole is based on unassuming, subtly evolved combinations of local areas of colour.

Meanwhile the hagiographical icon of *St Parasceve Piatnitsa*, which is of northern Tver provenance (Cat. Nos. 129—133), would appear to fuse the two currents of local archaism and common Russian tradition. The separate details in the marginal scenes are handled with elegance and an integrity of colour, combined with a lyrical refinement and expressiveness. Professional skill is here coupled with a simplicity of outlook. The craftsman who painted this intimate piece clearly had a fascination with the fifteenth-century tradition and persistently returned to solutions already employed — evidence of the second-hand, imitative nature of his art. The specifically sixteenth-century love of 'wordiness', of a detailed exegesis of the text illustrated, can be seen in abundant inscriptions covering every inch of spare space in the background of the marginal scenes. These were the work of a specialist artist, and are pieces of calligraphy, highly refined ones at that.

The few specimens of Tver illumination and the many icons indicate that towards the middle of the sixteenth century the relative integrity of Tver's artistic evolution had been succeeded by a definite degree of 'confusion'. Thus, the surviving works of this period include pieces oriented towards the central trends of post-Dionysian painting, such as a Deesis tier icon of the *Archangel Gabriel* (Cat. Nos. 134, 135) and such provincial items as a Deesis tier icon of the *Archangel Michael* and the illuminations of the *Book of the Four Gospels* donated in 1552 to the Zheltikov Monastery. Further, an icon of *St Anastasia, St Nicholas and the Apostle James* from Alexander Anisimov's collection (Cat. Nos. 137—139) represents an outburst of primitive archaism, virtually resurrecting fourteenth-century tradition, though the interpretation is largely of a superficial character.

However, the large icon of *St Ipatios of Gangra with Scenes from His Life* (Cat. Nos. 140—157) presents us with what is possibly the most striking example of a return to the archaic. Created no later than the mid-sixteenth century, its adherence to early Tver tradition is so fully and consistently expressed, especially in the marginal scenes, that it may be almost unreservedly considered to be associated with Tver, even though we do not know its exact provenance. The blend of expressiveness with immobile rigid forms in the figure in the centre is reminiscent of such examples of early local works as the *Archangel Michael* from the Anisimov collection and the Nektaryev Royal Doors (Cat. Nos. 8, 9; 25, 26). But particularly multifarious associations with fourteenth-century tradition are to be found in the marginal scenes illustrating the apocryphal *Seven Deaths of St Ipatios*. In the hands of this interpreter the narrative takes on a folkloristic tragic air. These scenes possess a tense dynamic character, even though they are seemingly empty and marked by a scattered presentation of the characters. The forms are simple, the painting colourful yet at the same time cool and restrained, while the manner of execution is highly expressive.

Apparently works of such power, deep emotionality and such a degree of archaism were few and far between, as the local course of evolution gradually receded in the face of the dominant trends of the time. Most painters had by now fully espoused the Muscovite aesthetic. Tver was drawn into the mainstream of Russian artistic development, its independence a thing of the past.

Even so, several striking pieces were created in Tver during this period. One is the small icon of *St Sabbatheus of Tver* (Cat. No. 136). Sabbatheus was a monk and contemporary of Agrephenius mentioned earlier, whose *Pilgrimage* is in Tver's Rogozhsky codex of the mid-fifteenth-century. Legend has it that Sabbatheus too went to Jerusalem. The icon depicts him praying in front of a cross on the bank of the Orsha River, one of tributaries of the Volga. Behind him we see his abode, a cave, the entrance to which, along with the fence, are traditionally conventional, as too is the manner in which the natural scenery has been handled — the usual approach to such wilderness scenes. As a whole the landscape is not without a certain elegance, the small trees and bushes with their smoothly curved branches are reminiscent of Muscovite icons of the first half of the sixteenth century, in which there is a stress on the bright and festive. The subject of the icon reflects the interest in the portrayal of figures from Russian history that had emerged in Russian art at the close of the fifteenth century. Such portraits were painted in particularly large numbers in the mid-sixteenth century. The detailed annotation in cinnabar is likewise characteristic of the period.

Perhaps the most indicative example of the espousal of Muscovite tradition by Tver artists is a small hagiographical icon of *St Nicholas with Scenes from His Life* (Cat. Nos. 159—161) of the 1560s from Tver's Church of the White Trinity. The work is remarkable for its radiant, vibrant and attractive colour scheme with plentiful gilding, and for the delicate handling of the miniature painting of the marginal scenes. Though far removed from the Muscovite icons of the Dionysian circle painted at the turn of the sixteenth century, its style ultimately derives from these icons. We can find echoes of them especially in the marginal scenes — just as in contemporary Muscovite painting and book illumination. A leaf from a set of Royal Doors depicting an Archangel and Evangelists (Cat. No. 158) represents a more provincialized version of the same trend.

In the second half of the sixteenth century Tver, like other Russian towns on the provincial periphery, invited artists from Moscow to create works that were commissioned in Tver's case by the local cathedral and noble landowners. After Ivan the Terrible's *oprichniks* ravaged the city in 1570, the influx of such artists and craftsmen must in all probability have increased. At any rate two notable icons were painted in Tver during this period.

One is an icon of the *Nativity of the Virgin with Scenes from Her Life* (Cat. Nos. 163—168), from the Isayevets Church in the suburbs of Tver, where once there was a village belonging to Muscovite landowners, who evidently commissioned the icon.

The icon's central part shows a complex panoramic view with a variety of architectural motifs which serve as coulisses dividing several scenes in which events separated in time take place; indeed the setting may be likened to panoramic depiction of a palace or even a whole town. Though this type of compositional arrangement was developed by Muscovite icon-painters in the middle of the sixteenth century and, especially in its second half, this work would appear to have achieved for the first time a scale imparting a sense of grandeur to episodes that are intimate by nature. In contrast to the complexity of the centrepiece, the surrounding marginal scenes are simple and straightforward in composition, but here too we find the increase in scale that had taken over from the delicate handling characteristic of immediate post-Dionysian art. The colour scheme is sombre on the whole, while the ponderous forms seem somehow clumsy. As we have already said, the icon undoubtedly belongs to the Muscovite tradition; however, it is hard to say whether its painter was a Muscovite or a provincial artist who had settled in Moscow. The artist may even have hailed from Pskov, as this city's craftsmen were held in particular favour at Ivan the Terrible's court in the mid-sixteenth century and later.

A man from Pskov was undoubtedly responsible for another major piece on a rare theme that was created in Tver in the third quarter of the sixteenth century — the *Portable Iconostasis* (Cat. No. 169) — most likely commissioned by Sabbas, Father Superior of the Pskov Monastery of the Caves, who was subsequently ordained Bishop of Tver. In all probability the artist who painted this small iconostasis came from Moscow at his invitation. The work incorporates a fascinating portrait-gallery of Russian statesmen and church dignitaries, the founders of notable monasteries, amidst whom Pskovian saints are the most fully represented.

Both the *Nativity of the Virgin* and the *Portable Iconostasis* markedly enrich our ideas of artistic activity in Tver in the second half of the sixteenth century. A contemporary example of the impact of the trend towards monumentalism, which

33. Annotated Gospel. 1530. From the Zheltikov Monastery. Tver Archives

34. The Service, Life and Eulogy of St Arsenius of Tver from the Zheltikov Monastery. 1665. Tver Archives

was distinctly manifest in Muscovite painting from the 1660s on, is presented by the
icon of *St Nicholas with Christ and the Virgin* from the Church of St Nicholas in the
Volhynia Quarter of Tver (Cat. Nos. 170, 171). In the execution of this imposing
image of great spiritual power, we may also discern a connection with the local
tendencies in art, although these are obviously on the decline. The culmination of
the local trend in Tver painting is the double-sided processional icon of the *Virgin
of the Sign* and *St Nicholas* from the Church of the White Trinity (Cat. Nos. 174,
175), which was painted either in the last few decades of the sixteenth century or at
the beginning of the seventeenth and already presents a frankly primitive type that
is fully in accordance with the provincial style of the period.

In Tver painting in the second half of the sixteenth century — alongside trends
reviewed — another style was also current sharing an affinity with the art of Yaroslavl, Nizhny Novgorod and other Volga towns, which was due to Tver's steady com-
mercial contacts with these places. Two examples of this trend are presented by the
Kashin icon of the *Miracle of St George and the Dragon* (Cat. No. 162) and an icon
on a relatively rare subject, i.e. *The Vernicle. Christ Entombed ('King of Glory')*
(Cat. No. 172), possibly produced in Tver itself. Both are vivid and colourful and
both attest to the regeneration of local art, though opening up a chapter that has no
connection whatever with the previous evolution of art in Tver.

Unfortunately later seventeenth-century Tver painting has hardly been studied
at all — due to the circumstance that many works produced there need to be freed
of overpainting while many other icons were lost owing to the countless fires, repairs
and rebuilding of Tver's churches in the eighteenth and nineteenth centuries.

Throughout the seventeenth century royal icon-painters from the Kremlin
Armoury often travelled to Tver and neighbouring towns to work there. At the same
time works by Russia's leading artists were being sent to the city, as, for instance, the
Moses the Hungarian, Prince Vladimir and Arcadius Novotorzhsky (painted in
1677 by Simon Ushakov and Grigory Zinovyev). Muscovite craftsmen decorated the
Cathedral of the Transfiguration in 1696 and the Kashin Cathedral (Cat. Nos. 27—
33). The best manuscripts in local monasterial and church libraries from this period
were of Muscovite origin — as is demonstrated by a synodicon of 1665 from the Zhel-

tikov Monastery that incorporates the *Service, Life and Eulogy of St Arsenius of Tver* and the richly illuminated 1685 *Synodicon* from the same monastery (ills. 34, 35).

During the first few decades of the seventeenth century Tver art gradually declined. The greatest interest amongst pieces known to have been produced at this time is evoked by the small door to the prothesis of Tver's Church of the Dormition, which is adorned with two scenes, the *Expulsion from Paradise* and the *Parable of the Blind Man and the Lame Man* (Cat. No. 173). Though simple and unpretentious, the painting is rather fine and warm, with the style still revealing tangible traces of late sixteenth-century traditions.

As for other pieces, which are chiefly from around Tver and also from more distant parts of the former Tver principality, they demonstrate the obvious links with the painting of the Volga towns which was mentioned earlier (Cat. Nos. 176, 177; 178, 179).

As far as we can judge there was a certain degree of artistic revival in Tver in the final decades of the seventeenth century. Again, as archive documents and inscriptions on works of applied art show, it was mostly the local merchant classes and the church that commissioned these new pieces, as had been the case in the sixteenth century. Many precious items for both secular and church use were contrived. One is the 1687 chalice featuring portraits of Bishop Arsenius and Prince Mikhail Yaroslavich from the Cathedral of the Transfiguration (ill. 36). Such portraiture was rather rare on articles of applied arts, but in late seventeenth-century Tver icons it became a favourite theme.

Thus, one of the more remarkable pieces of this type is the icon of *Prince Mikhail Yaroslavich and Xenia of Tver*, painted in the 1690s, from the sacristy of the Cathedral of the Transfiguration (Cat. Nos. 180, 181). These two portrayals call to mind the frontispiece illumination of the *Chronicle of Georgius Hamartolos* (ill. 4), and are important evidence of the endurance of the local tradition. The landscape between the two figures is almost realistic, yet abstractly symbolical. But interest is chiefly aroused by the depiction of the city that these two saints are protecting — though conventional, this view of Tver is topographically accurate as well as being painstakingly and affectionately painted.

Another icon, created like the chalice in 1687, depicts Bishop Arsenius and Prince Mikhail Yaroslavich (Cat. No. 182). Though the prince's portrait greatly resembles the one on the icon described above, on the whole this monument belongs to a different iconographic tradition. In the centre there is a view of Tver with the Cathedral of the Transfiguration and its bell-tower with a gate-tower and bridge in front. We may note the very special attention paid to the view and to the "Transfiguration", presented as if seen by the bishop and the prince in a vision. The view of the city has a spatial quality and visual verisimilitude, combined with a more pronounced

36. The Sainted Bishop Arsenius and Grand Prince Mikhail Yaroslavich of Tver. 1687. Detail of the chalice from the Cathedral of the Transfiguration of the Saviour in Tver. Museum of History, Architecture and Literature, Tver

decorativeness of forms. The manner of treatment has much in common with the icons produced at the Kremlin Armoury in Moscow, Russia's leading art centre throughout the second half of the seventeenth century and the early Petrine period. The refined traditionalism of the icon depicting Mikhail and his mother Xenia has now yielded to an emphatic sumptuousness. In evidence too are indications of the style that is characteristic of the transitional epoch.

In short this icon is the fullstop, as it were, to the artistic development of ancient Tver. Works of traditional form continued to be produced here later, such as the hagiographical icon of *St Simeon the Stylite*, painted about 1718 for the church of the same name (it is now in the Andrei Rublev Museum in Moscow), but they were already of only secondary significance in the art scene of the period.

Though there is no question that following the restoration of numerous other pieces our conception of the concluding phase of Tver's artistic development will be substantially enriched and refined, we may state that neither the sixteenth nor the seventeenth century saw the zenith of art in the city, Tver's real contribution to the treasure-trove of medieval Russian culture. The most important periods in this respect were the end of the thirteenth century, the first few decades of the fourteenth century and the turn of the fifteenth century, with Tver's artistic development reaching its peak in the mid-fifteenth century. The strikingly unique works of icon-painting and other genres which were produced in those times have ensured Tver's place in the history of early Russian painting. To fully assess the history of medieval Russian art, it is essential to have a knowledge of the artistic legacy of Tver which spans the early period when the Russian national tradition was emerging within the conditions of the yoke of the Golden Horde and the time of flourishing in the fifteenth century.

PLATES

3

4

12. THE VIRGIN HODEGETRIA. Obverse of the
processional icon. First quarter of the 15th century
13. Detail of No. 12

15. THE NATIVITY OF THE VIRGIN. Obverse of the
processional icon. First half of the 15th century. Fragment:
Maidens

18. ST JOHN THE BAPTIST. From a Deesis tier. First half
of the 15th century
19. Detail of No. 18

20. THE NATIVITY OF THE VIRGIN. First half of the
15th century
21. The Washing of the Infant Virgin. Detail of No. 20
22. St Anne with Maidens. Detail of No. 20

БЧА

24. THE VIRGIN HODEGETRIA. First half or middle of
the 15th century

25. Royal Doors. Left Leaf: ST JOHN CHRYSOSTOM. Right leaf:
ST BASIL THE GREAT. First half of the 15th century.

26. Half-length Figure of St John Chrysostom. Detail of the
left-hand leaf of No. 25

ІѠАЛАСТ҃Ъ

26

27. CHRIST IN MAJESTY. From a Deesis tier. Second
quarter or middle of the 15th century
28. Detail of No. 27
29. Right Hand of Christ. Detail of No. 27
30. Angel, Emblem of the Evangelist Matthew.
Detail of No. 27

31. Eagle, Emblem of the Evangelist St John the Divine.
Detail of No. 27
32. Lion, Emblem of the Evangelist Mark. Detail of No. 27
33. Ox, Emblem of the Evangelist Luke. Detail of No. 27

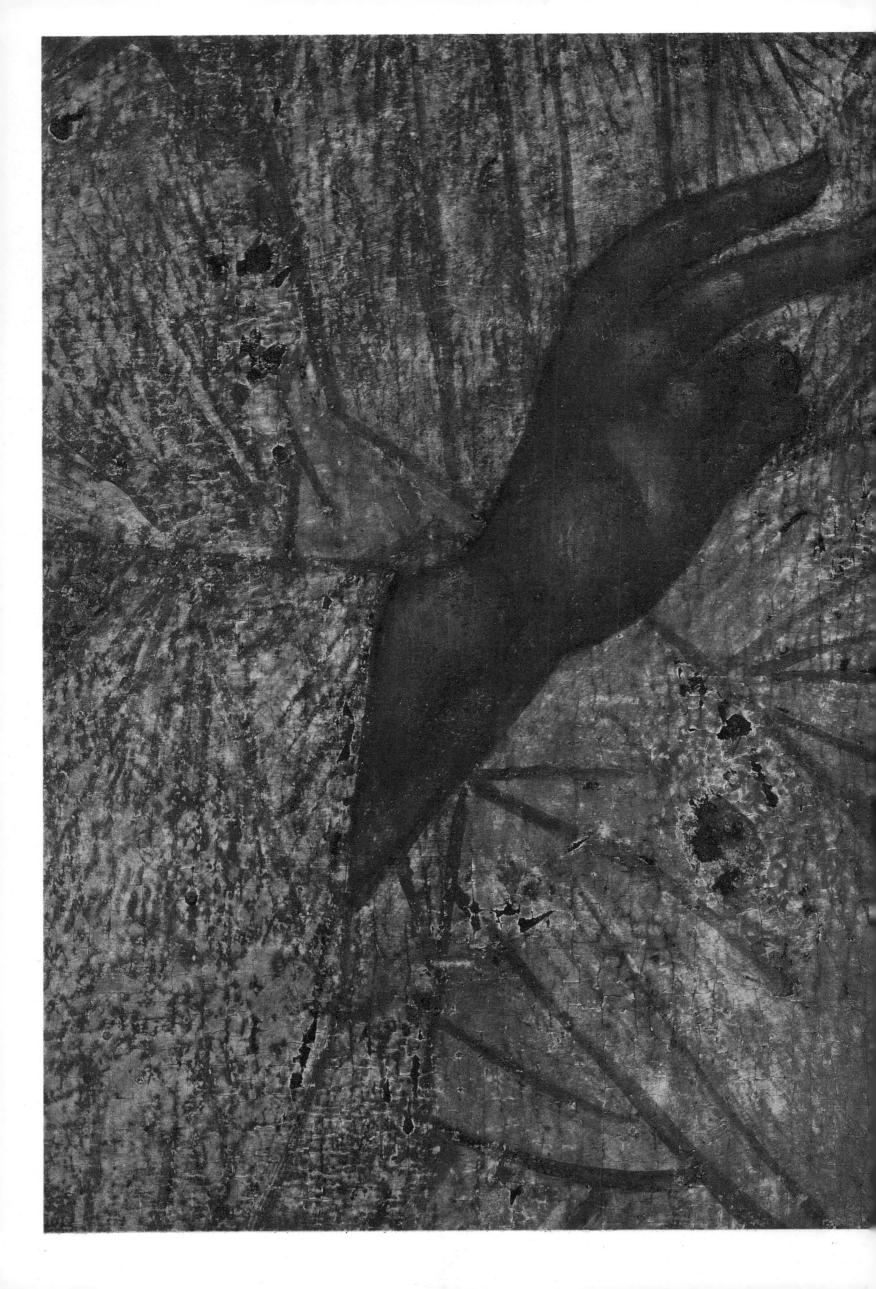

34. THE ARCHANGEL MICHAEL. From a Deesis tier.
Second quarter or middle of the 15th century
35. Detail of No. 34

36. THE ARCHANGEL GABRIEL. From a Deesis tier.
Second quarter or middle of the 15th century
37. Detail of No. 36

38. THE NATIVITY OF CHRIST. From a Church Feasts
tier. Second quarter or middle of the 15th century
39. St Joseph and the Magi. Detail of No. 38
40. The Virgin and the Infant in the Manger. Detail of No. 38
41. The Washing of the Infant. Detail of No. 38
42. Sheep. Detail of No. 38
43. Group of Angels. Detail of No. 38

НАШЕ ІСХС

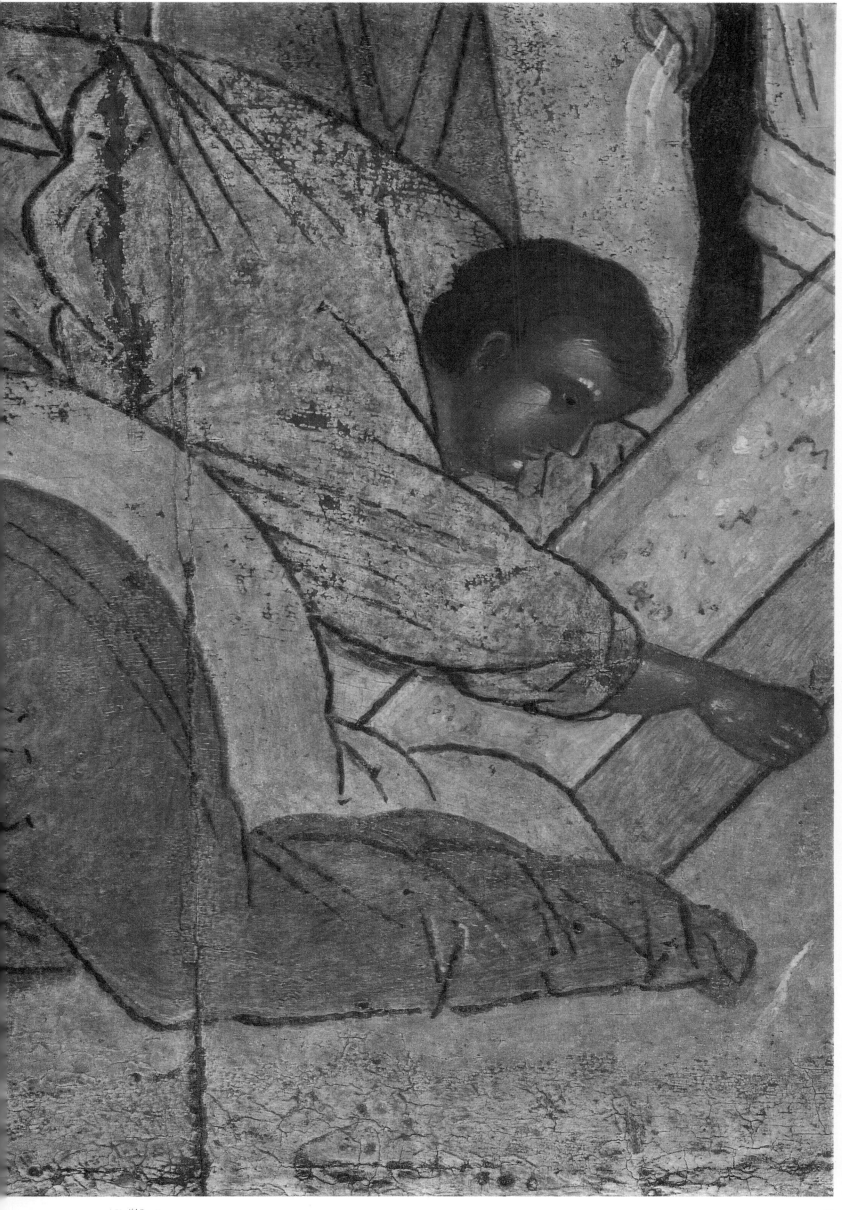

53. THE ENTRY INTO JERUSALEM. From a Church
Feasts tier. Second quarter or middle of the 15th century
54. Welcoming Group. Detail of No. 53
55. Panoramic View of the City. Detail of No. 53

54

56. THE BAPTISM OF CHRIST. From a Church Feasts
tier. Second quarter or middle of the 15th century
57. Group of Angels. Detail of No. 56

58. THE ASCENSION. From a Church Feasts tier. Second
quarter or middle of the 15th century
59. Group of Apostles with Angel. Detail of No. 58
60. Christ Within the Sphere. Detail of No. 58

59

НШЕ ІС ХС

61. THE DESCENT OF THE HOLY GHOST. From a
Church Feasts tier. Second quarter or middle of the 15th
century
62. Group of Apostles. Detail of No. 61

65. KING DAVID. From a Prophets tier. Second quarter or
middle of the 15th century

67. THE PROPHET EZEKIEL. From a Prophets tier. Second
quarter or middle of the 15th century

68. **THE PATRIARCH JACOB.** From a Prophets tier. Second
quarter or middle of the 15th century

69. CHRIST IN MAJESTY. From a Deesis tier. 15th century
70. Detail of No. 69
71. Angel, Emblem of the Evangelist Matthew.
Detail of No. 69
72. Eagle, Emblem of St John the Divine. Detail of No. 69

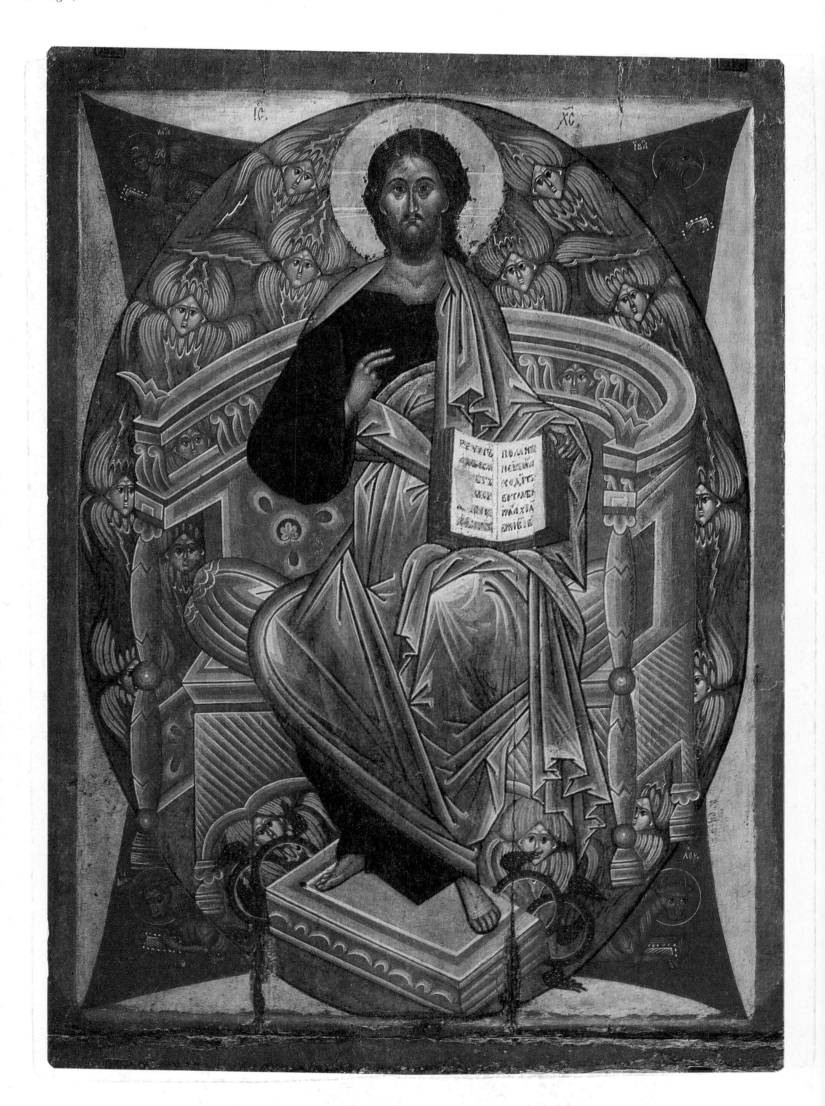

72

73. THE VIRGIN. From a Deesis tier. 15th century
74. Detail of No. 73

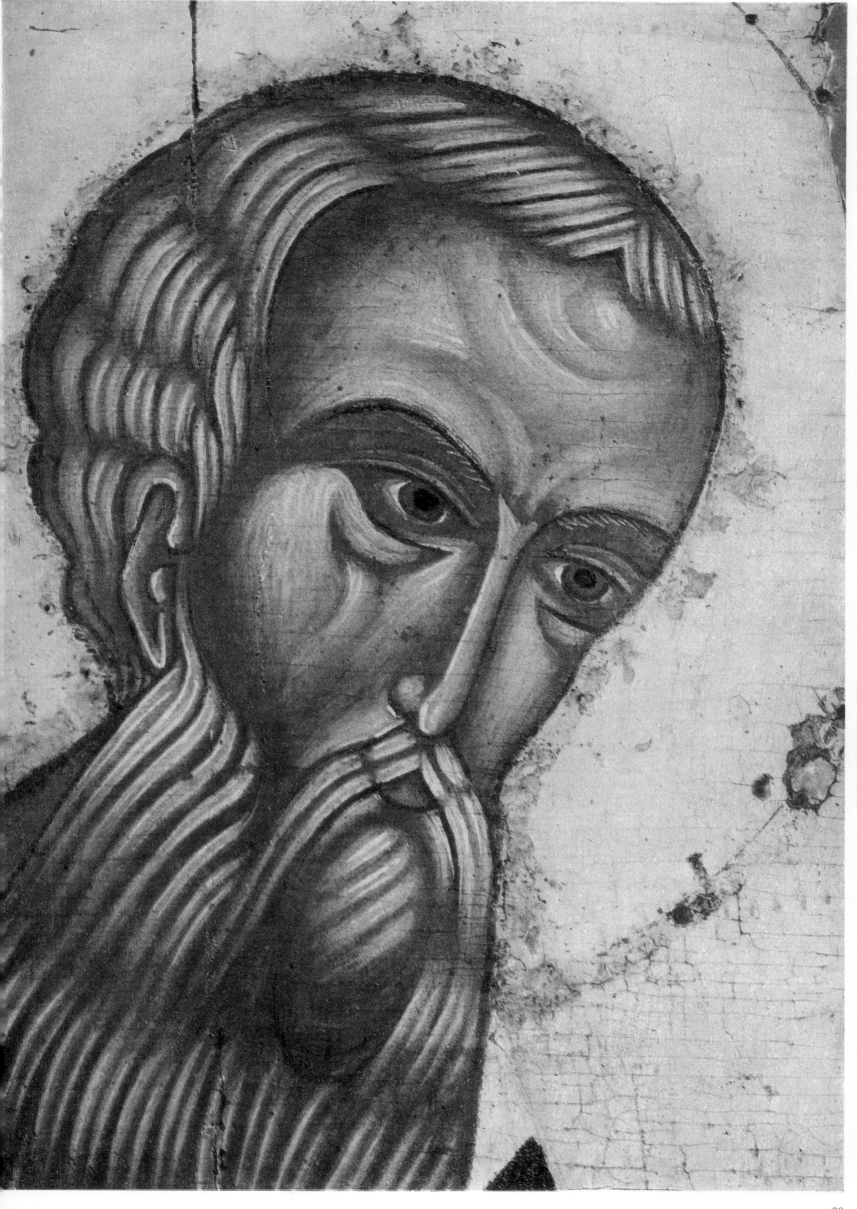

83. ST DEMETRIUS OF THESSALONICA. From a Deesis
tier. 15th century

91. THE SYNAXIS (LAUDATION) OF THE VIRGIN.
Second half of the 15th century
92. Shepherds. Detail of No. 91
93. St John Damascene and the Globe. Detail of No. 91
94. Singers. Detail of No. 91

93

97. ST JOHN THE BAPTIST. From a Deesis tier. Second
half of the 15th century
98. Detail of No. 97
99. Detail of No. 97
100. Detail of No. 97

101. THE OLD TESTAMENT TRINITY.
1484—85. By master Paisii
102. Half-length Figure of the Central Angel. Detail of
No. 101
103. Abraham's Chambers and the Mamre Oak. Detail of
No. 101

102

105. Royal Doors. Left-leaf scene: THE EVANGELIST LU-
KE AND SANCTA SOPHIA THE HOLY WISDOM. Second
half of the 15th century

114. CHRIST PANTOCRATOR. From a Deesis tier. Last
quarter of the 15th century
115. Detail of No. 114
116. Detail of No. 114

115

117. THE APOSTLE PAUL. From a Deesis tier. Last
quarter of the 15th century
118. Detail of No. 117

124

127. **ST JOHN THE ALMSGIVER.** From a Deesis tier. First
third of the 16th century
128. Detail of No. 127

128

132

134. THE ARCHANGEL GABRIEL. From a Deesis tier.
First half of the 16th century
135. Detail of No. 134

135

141

143

144

148

153

154

159. ST NICHOLAS WITH SCENES FROM HIS LIFE.
Ca. 1560s
160. Novitiate. Marginal scene 3 from No. 159
161. The Burial of St Nicholas. Marginal scene 13 from No. 159

173. Door to a Prothesis. Scenes: THE EXPULSION FROM
PARADISE; THE PARABLE OF THE LAME MAN AND
THE BLIND MAN. First half of the 17th century.

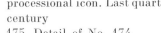

174. THE VIRGIN OF THE SIGN. Obverse of the
processional icon. Last quarter of the 16th or early 17th
century
175. Detail of No. 174

176. THE NATIVITY OF THE VIRGIN. First half of the
17th century. By a Volga Region artist
177. Detail of No. 176

178. ST NICHOLAS WITH SCENES FROM HIS LIFE.
Second half of the 17th century. By a Volga Region artist
179. St Nicholas Appears in a Dream to Emperor
Constantine. Marginal scene 7 from No. 178

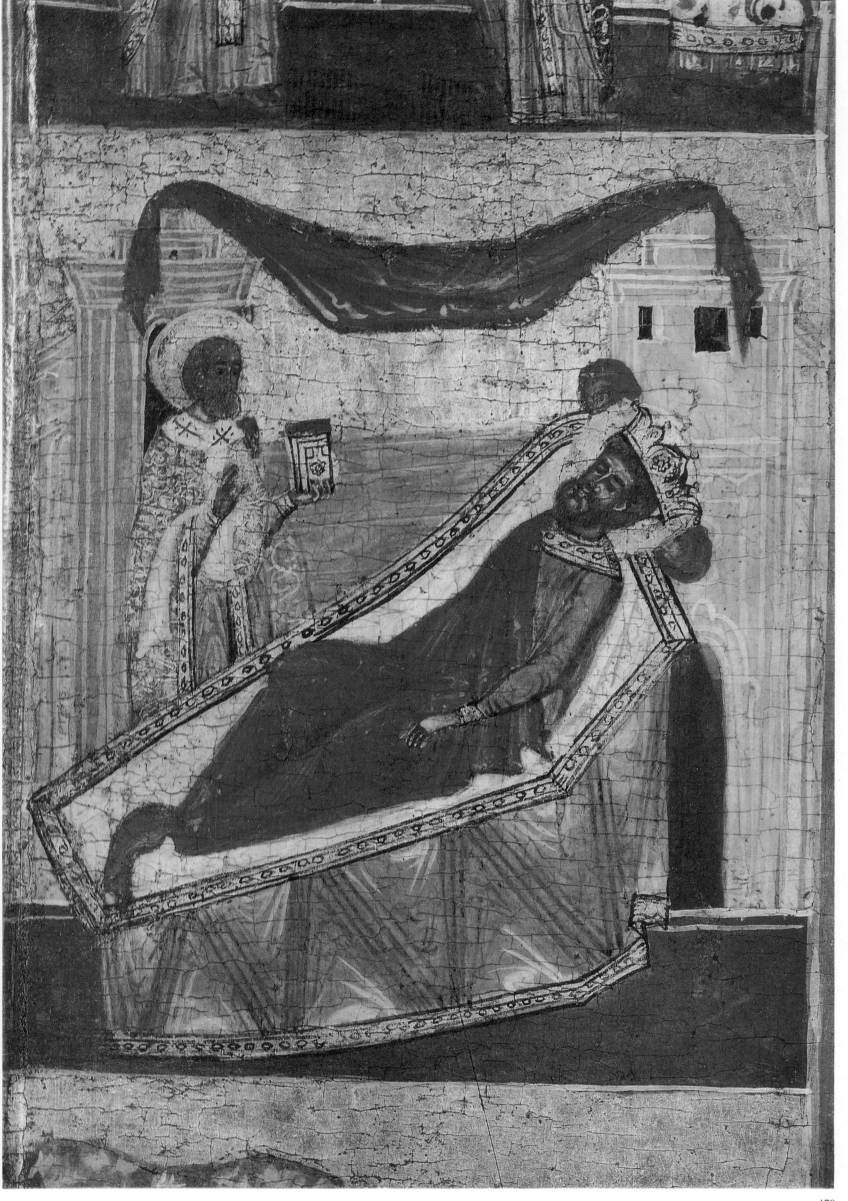

181

CATALOGUE

Explanatory Notes

The present catalogue includes icons painted between the second half of the thirteenth century and the seventeenth century, which have been attributed to Tver mainly by virtue of their style. In most cases this stylistic affinity has been confirmed by evidence of their provenance either from Tver or from the various cities, towns and territories of the Principality of Tver. While the attributions offered here in the majority of cases accord with established tradition, some icons have been given more precise datings and their place in the evolution of the Tver icon has been appropriately clarified. The reader will also find in this catalogue several known icons which have previously been attributed to other artistic centres. The new attribution, while being proposed in some cases without reservations, is in others purely a hypothesis. Virtually the entire body of Tver icons from the thirteenth to fifteenth centuries, with the exception of icons particularly ravaged by time or unhappily restored, plus most of the sixteenth-century works freed of overpaint, are presented here. Many seventeenth-century icons are still awaiting restoration. In addition to later icons of Tver origin, the catalogue also includes works produced in Tver by icon-painters from elsewhere.

Measurements are given in centimetres throughout with height preceding width. The thickness of the panel is not indicated, nor do we specify the wood which is mostly limewood or some softwood. Since all the icons presented were painted in egg tempera on wood — which as a rule is covered with a strip of canvas (*pavoloka*) and a gesso grounding (*levkas*) — no description is given of either the medium or the technique employed. On the other hand, information is furnished as to the state of preservation, the iconography and the provenance. Wherever necessary, additional information is provided with regard to attribution and considerations are voiced as to the reliability of an attribution or affinity with some other artistic tradition, should the icon have been produced in Tver by a painter from some other centre. Inscriptions and legends on icons are only referred to, if they provide some historical data. Each annotation is furnished with a bibliography and a list of exhibitions at which the icons listed have been shown.

1—5. SS BORIS AND GLEB
Second half of the 13th century; renovated in the first third of the 14th century

154×104

Museum of Russian Art, Kiev

Inv. No. Ж-1

State of preservation: Patchy. The upper layers of the initial modelling were partially lost as early as the icon's first renovation which took place approximately in the first third of the fourteenth century. The remains of a paint layer from the second half of the thirteenth century can be discerned beneath the highlights (*probela*) added in the early fourteenth century. (The left hand of Prince Boris is in the best state of preservation.) The technique employed in the execution of the 'initial' layer and its general typology derive from the imitation of an earlier prototype. This icon is most probably a replica of a prototype from the twelfth or early thirteenth century. There are also traces of restoration carried out in the first half of the fifteenth century (patches of the red ground with lettering), in the sixteenth century and in the seventeenth or early eighteenth century. The 1914 restoration introduced a substantial amount of touching up, including some additional ornamentation echoing old forms.

Iconography: The two princes Boris and Gleb, whose feast-days are May 2/15 (the first date is according to the Old Style Julian calendar still used by the Orthodox Church) and July 24/August 6, were renamed Roman and David at their baptism. They were sons of Prince Vladimir and brothers of Yaroslav the Wise and were murdered around 1015 during a period of internecine strife. They are Russia's first two saints having been officially canonized no later than 1072. During the eleventh century representations of them could be found on princely seals, with the names Roman and David, and on reliquary crucifixes. From the twelfth century they were portrayed either as warrior saints or as martyred princes, the oldest extant painted depiction being in the early twelfth-century frescoes of the Good Friday Church in Polotsk. Towards the close of the century, these two versions fused with the two brothers represented each holding a cross and a sword and wearing the typical princely dress of hat and cloak, and it is this iconography that can be seen here (* V. I. Lesiuchevsky, "The Vyshgorod Cult of Boris and Gleb in Relics",

---

* Here and further all publications marked by an asterisk are in Russian.

Soviet Archaeology, vol. 8, Moscow — Leningrad, 1946; Smirnova 1976, pp. 178—180; Popov 1979, pp. 255—258).

Provenance: From the Vishera Monastery of St Sabbatheus in Novgorod. In about 1914 it was acquired by the Kiev collector V. Kharitonenko. Subsequently, between 1930 and 1934 it was in the possession of various state museums. Since 1935 it has been in the Kiev Museum of Russian Art. It is tentatively suggested that the icon was brought from Tver to the Vishera Monastery by its founder St Sabbatheus of Vishera, a member of a noble family of the Tver area, the Borozdins. According to the available historical information, this man played a considerable role in the religious life of Tver in the late fourteenth century. His founding of the monastery on Novgorodian territory around 1420 coincided with the start of extensive construction and artistic work in Tver during the reign of Grand Prince Boris Alexandrovich. The manner of painting displays greater affinity with the traditions of North-Eastern Russia, not those of Novgorod.

The cult of the two saints, Boris and Gleb, was popular with the local princes and aristocracy from earliest times (ill. 3 in the text). It is quite possible that the icon was originally in Tver's first church of SS Cosmas and Damian where the first Grand Prince, Yaroslav Vsevolodovich, was buried in 1271. On the other hand, the icon could have been specially painted for the Cathedral of the Transfiguration of Our Saviour (1285—89) which was erected in place of the above-named church. To judge by its name, there was some definite link with the first church that the Kievan Prince Vladimir Monomachus erected in Vladimir in 1108. The reverence shown by the Tver princely dynasty for the two brothers was likewise linked to the traditions of Vladimir and, in part, to those of Kiev: the remains of SS Boris and Gleb were interred in Vyshgorod outside Kiev, while the church built by Yury Dolgoruky (The Long-armed) in 1152 and consecrated to these two saints was located in his royal village of Kideksha near Suzdal, the second centre of the Principality of Vladimir-Suzdal. In the eyes of the princes of Tver, with their political ambitions, Boris and Gleb were above all the 'family saints'.

Exhibitions: 1969—70 Moscow

References: * Archimandrite Macarius, *An Archaeological Description of Ecclesiastical Antiquities in Novgorod* and *Its Environs*, vol. 1, Moscow, 1858, pp. 628, 630; V. I. Lesiuchevsky, *op. cit.*; Smirnova 1976, pp. 178— 180; Popov 1979, pp. 255—258; * *Kiev Museum of Russian Art. Catalogue*, 1955, p. 9, ill.; * *Kiev Museum of Russian Art. Guide*, 1955, p. 10; * V. N. Lazarev, *The Frescoes of Old Ladoga*, Moscow, 1960, p. 41; Onasch 1961, pl. 20, pp. 353, 354; * N. N. Chernogubov, "The Icon of SS Boris and Gleb in the Kiev Museum of Russian Art", in: *Early Russian Art of the 15th and Early 16th Centuries*, Moscow, 1963, pp. 285—290, ill. between p. 286 and p. 287; * N. V. Pertsev, "Concerning Certain Methods of Facial Portrayal in Early Russian Easel Painting. 12th—13th Century", *Transactions of the State Russian Museum*, Leningrad, 1964, issue 13, p. 90; V. A. Bogusevich, L. S. Miliayeva, "Easel Painting", in: *The History of Ukrainian Art* (in Ukrainian), vol. 1, Kiev, 1966, p. 336, pl. 268; Lazarev 1969, pp. 17, 18; Tver Painting 1970, p. 14 (No. 1); Popov 1970, pp. 314, 316; Yevseyeva, Kochetkov, Sergeyev 1974, pp. 9, 10, pls. 1—3 (Idem 1983); Smirnova 1976, pp. 178—180, ill. p. 179; Popov 1978, pp. 184, 185, ill. p. 183; Popov 1979, pp. 34—41, 252—259, ills. pp. 371—375; Lazarev 1983, pp. 130, 502 (No. 140); * S. I. Golubev, L. N. Pelkina, "Studies of the Icon of *SS Boris and Gleb* from the Kiev Museum of Russian Art", in: *Problems of the Comprehensive Study of Art Museums. The Russian Museum. Collection of Scholarly Papers*, Leningrad, 1986, pp. 100—104

6, 7. CHRIST PANTOCRATOR
14th century

108×81

Tretyakov Gallery, Moscow
Inv. No. 15028

State of preservation: Considerable losses of priming and the original paint layer with remains of later renovations and touchings up introduced during subsequent restoration.

Iconography: The half-length portrayal of Christ in benediction, holding a closed Gospel is traditional and belongs to a type popular in Byzantine and Russian art (Kondakov 1905, pp. 61—63; K. Wessel, "Christusbild", in: *Reallexikon*, vol. 1, 1965, issue 7, col. 966—1047; and especially col. 1014—1017). Found in Russian icons from the thirteenth century, this iconographic version became widespread from the fourteenth century, as evidenced by extant icons of Pskovian and Novgorodian provenance. Such icons often form the centrepiece of a Deesis tier. Equally common were single-figure portrayals destined for the lower, local tier of iconostases or for special cases. It is not clear what this particular icon was originally intended for.

8, 9. THE ARCHANGEL MICHAEL
Turn of the 15th century

87×84

Tretyakov Gallery, Moscow
Inv. No. 15030

Provenance: From the collection of the art historian and restorer A. I. Anisimov. Acquired by the Tretyakov Gallery in 1931. Oral tradition ascribes it to Tver province and the style of the icon supports this. In the 1920s Anisimov paid many visits to Tver and the surrounding region and his collection is known to have included several locally painted icons from the fourteenth to sixteenth centuries (Cat. Nos. 8, 9; 69—86).

Exhibitions: 1958 Moscow; 1960 Moscow; 1969—70 Moscow

References: Kondakov 1905, pp. 61—63; Olsufyev 1935, p. 28, and 1936, p. 47; Rublev Exhibition. Catalogue 1960, pp. 18, 25 (No. 3); Antonova, Mneva 1963, 1, p. 232, No. 197, ills. 135, 136; Lazarev 1965, p. 70; Vzdornov 1970, p. 271, ill. p. 272; Tver Painting 1970, p. 15 (No. 2); Popov 1970, pp. 314—317; Vagner 1974, p. 196; Yevseyeva, Kochetkov, Sergeyev 1974, pp. 14, 15, pls. 6, 7; Idem. 1983, p. 13; Smirnova 1976, p. 214; Popov 1978, pp. 185, 188, ill. p. 186; Popov 1979, pp. 41—48, ill. p. 376; Lazarev 1983, p. 130

State of preservation: Uneven. Abraded priming and paint layer in places with subsequent additions, especially in the lower portion as a result of repairs made to the panel. Also traces of repairs of the sixteenth and seventeenth centuries.

Iconography: The full-face portrayal of the Archangel is known in Byzantine and early Russian art, chiefly in two variants. In one variant the Archangel is dressed in a courtly Byzantine style, usually holding an orb and sceptre. In the other variant he is depicted as a warrior, the supreme commander of the Heavenly Host. The second variant can be found in Russian icons from the thirteenth century, reaching a high point in fifteenth- and sixteenth-century painting and sculpture. The pose and gestures are traditional for the representation of warriors in Byzantine art and in Russian art from the eleventh to the fifteenth century (Cat. Nos. 34, 35).

Provenance: Similar to Cat. Nos. 6, 7

Exhibitions: 1960 Moscow; 1969—70 Moscow

References: * O. S. Popova, *The Art of Novgorod and Muscovy in the First Half of the Fourteenth Century. Its Links with Byzantium*, Moscow, 1980, p. 223 (note 16); Rublev Exhibition. Catalogue 1960, p. 31 (No. 27); Antonova, Mneva 1963, I, p. 233, No. 198, ill. 137; Vzdornov 1970, p. 271; Painting of Ancient Tver 1970, p. 16 (No. 4); Popov 1970, pp. 317, 318, 320; Yevseyeva, Kochetkov, Sergeyev 1974, pp. 16, 17, pls. 8, 9; Idem 1983, pp. 14, 15; Popov 1979, pp. 66—70 and 262—264, ills. pp. 67, 377

10, 11. ST BARBARA
Early 15th century. Tver (?)

73×50
Tretyakov Gallery, Moscow
Inv. No. 25518

State of preservation: Good on the whole, but considerable losses of the priming and paint layer in the lower portion and the margins.

Iconography: St Barbara whose feast-day is December 4/17 was martyred according to legend by pagans in Heliopolis about 306 A.D. during the reign of the Emperor Maximian. Other sources, however, date her martyrdom earlier, to the third century. The cult became popular in Constantinople at the turn of the tenth century, and in Kiev from the late eleventh century (Sergius 1876, part 1, pp. 320, 321; part 2, pp. 377, 378). Depictions of her are relatively rare in early art; thus only two miniatures of her have been found in eleventh-century Greek Menologies (P. Mijović, *Menolog*, Belgrade, 1973, p. 195, note 146; p. 202, note 163, in Serbian). Apart from the customary cross of martyrdom the distinguishing iconographic feature is a crown, since according to legend the saint was of a noble, 'kingly' family.

Though the oldest depiction in Russian painting with accompanying inscription is now to be found in the frescoes of the 1199 Church of Our Saviour on the Nereditsa near Novgorod, it is quite possible that a similar image was already in existence in the mid-eleventh century in St Sophia's, Kiev (compare the unnamed figure wearing something like a crown in G. N. Logvin, *St Sophia's in Kiev*, Kiev, 1971, ill. 131, in Ukrainian). The present icon is the oldest known Russian icon on this theme. In other fifteenth-century works the saint is represented among a group of female martyrs. In the sixteenth century we find many different ways of depicting this saint.

Provenance: According to information supplied by collectors, P. P. Shebanov took this icon from Uglich in 1910. Before it was acquired by the Tretyakov Gallery in 1940, it changed hands among private collectors more than once. In all likelihood the fact that the icon turned up in Uglich was a consequence of the activities of Old Believers. Indeed, two other fifteenth-century icons were found in the local chapel (Cat. Nos. 95, 96; 97—100) together with a large number of other old icons of varying provenance. Some were acquired by the Tretyakov Gallery, others are in the possession of the Uglich Museum. Despite this work's undoubted similarity to Tver icons (Cat. Nos. 12—14), the proposed attribution is still to some extent conjectural.

Exhibitions: 1957 Warsaw; 1967 Moscow, Tretyakov Gallery

References: * V. N. Lazarev, *The Art of Novgorod*, Moscow — Leningrad, 1947, p. 94; * M. V. Alpatov, *The General History of Art*, vol. 3, Moscow, 1955, p. 211, pl. 126; Malarstwo rosyjskie XIV—XX w. 1957, p. 36 (No. 1); Alpatow 1958 (*Ibid.* 1962), pp. 24, 29, ill. 34; * N. V. Shchepkina, *14th-century Bulgarian Illuminations. The Study of the Tomich Psalter*, Moscow, 1963, p. 60, ill. p. 59; Rostov-Suzdalian Painting 1967, p. 88 (No. 32); * L. Bolshakova, E. Kamenskaya, *The State Tretyakov Gallery*, Moscow, 1968, p. 22, ill. 14; Rozanova 1970, No. 52; Smirnova, Laurina, Gordiyenko 1982. p. 176; M. V. Alpatov, *Treasures of Russian Art in the 11th—16th Centuries*, Leningrad, 1971, p. 23, pl. 161

12—14. DOUBLE-SIDED ICON OF THE VIRGIN HODEGETRIA AND ST NICHOLAS
First quarter of the 15th century

56×40.5 (without 7.5 cm long handle)
Rublev Museum of Early Russian Art, Moscow
Inv. No КП 549

State of preservation: Uneven. Considerable losses of the priming on the obverse, filled in during restoration. Heavy losses in the margins on the reverse. On the whole minor losses and abrasion of the paint layer.

Iconography: There are several highly revered icons of the Virgin of the Hodegetria type. The most popular in Russia in the fifteenth century was the Smolensk Hodegetria, whose feast-day is July 28/August 10. However, while bearing the Balkan prototype in mind, it is unlikely that we are dealing with a replica here. The variant is traditional and does not warrant our identifying this icon with any particular Byzantine or Southern Slavonic original. The portrayal of St Nicholas who was the Bishop of Myra in Lycia on the Mediterranean coast of Asia Minor in the fourth century (his feast-day is December 6/19 and the translation of his relics to Bari in Italy in 1087 is recalled on May 9/22) is also quite traditional. Both representations are typical of fourteenth- and fifteenth-century two-sided processional icons. (For types of such icons see the articles by A. Grabar and A. Ksingopulos in *Cahiers archéologiques*, X, 1959 and XII, 1962; Smirnova 1976, pp. 243—245).

Provenance: From the Church of St Basil the Great in the village of Vasilyevskoye near Staritsa. Acquired by the Rublev Museum in 1967.

Exhibitions: 1968 Moscow; 1969—70 Moscow; 1972 Moscow; Byzantium — the Balkans — Early Russia. Icons of the 13th— First Half of the 15th Century. Moscow, Tretyakov Gallery, 1991

References: Tver Painting 1970, p. 23 (No. 15); Popov 1969/1970, pp. 315—322; Popov 1970, p. 344, ill. p. 345; Vagner, Kukles, Tikhomirova 1972, pp. 93, 94, ill. 7; Briusova 1974, pp. 186, 187, note 30; Yevseyeva, Kochetkov, Sergeyev 1974, pp. 20, 21, pls. 13, 14; Idem 1983, pp. 16, 17; Smirnova 1976, p. 244; Popov 1978, p. 191; Popov 1979, pp. 112—120ff, ills. pp. 380—382; Saltykov 1981, pp. 15, 242, ill. pp. 12—14; Popov 1982, p. 309, fig. 7; Lazarev 1983, p. 146 (note 289) * *Byzantium — the Balkans — Early Russia. Icons of the 13th— First Half of the 15th Century. Exhibition Catalogue* (ed. by L. Livshits), Moscow, 1991, pp. 292, 293, Cat. No. 90

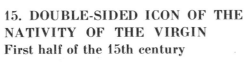

15. DOUBLE-SIDED ICON OF THE NATIVITY OF THE VIRGIN
First half of the 15th century

64×45 (without 52 cm long handle)
Rublev Museum of Early Russian Art, Moscow
Inv. No. КП 643

State of preservation: The painting on the obverse is patchy and much of the priming is missing. However, the extant sections are in a relatively good state of preservation. The reverse carries painting done in the nineteenth century.

Iconography: The subject matter is from the *Protevangelium of St James the Less* (V, 2), with the basic elements of the composition having finalized by the eleventh—twelfth centuries. Essential iconographic details have in the present icon been partly reconstructed on the basis of small surviving remnants — they include the figure of the servant-woman supporting St Anne from the back — which is found in Byzantine painting from the twelfth century — and also the portrayal of St Joachim and the cradle episode in the lower right-hand corner which can be found in icon-painting from the early fourteenth century. The present full iconographic version is quite possibly the earliest in Russian icon-painting (for literary sources see Porfiryev 1890, pp. 10—12, 136—164; and for the most fully studied iconography, Lafontaine-Dosogne 1964—1965, I, pp. 89—121; II, pp. 215, 216). This icon belongs to the relatively common processional type, which depicted the Virgin, Christ or some sacred or Gospel subject, and often the Annunciation or another scene from the life of the Virgin. However, no other processional icons depicting the Nativity of the Virgin are known. (For their list see Smirnova 1976, p. 243, note 4.)

Provenance: See Cat. Nos. 12—14. Acquired by the Rublev Museum in 1968.

Exhibitions: 1969—70 Moscow; 1972 Moscow

References: Tver Painting 1970, pp. 23, 24 (No. 16); Popov 1970, p. 344; Yevseyeva, Kochetkov, Sergeyev 1974, pp. 22, 23, pl. 22 (*Ibid.* 1983, p. 19); Popov 1978, p. 191; Popov 1979, pp. 120—123ff, 273—275, ills. pp. 121, 383

16, 17. THE VIRGIN
From a half-length Deesis tier.
First half of the 15th century
80×57.5
Rublev Museum of Early Russian Art, Moscow
Inv. No КП 441

State of preservation: Satisfactory on the whole, with the exception of losses of the priming in the lower part of the icon which have been filled in and touched up during restoration. There is also considerable abrasion of the paint layer, crackling and partially eroded glazings on the face and hands.

Iconography: The Deesis tier, or simply Deesis, appeared in Christian art no later than the seventh century and originally incorporated icons of *Christ Pantocrator*, the *Virgin* and *St John the Baptist* (Cat. Nos. 18, 19). Subsequently the composition broadened (Th. V. Bogyay, "Deesis", in: *Reallexikon*, 1968, vol. II, issue 8, col. 1179—1182). This particular icon presents a variant common in fourteenth- and fifteenth-century Byzantine and Russian icon-painting of half-length, or seated (as they were termed in old Russian inventories), Deesis tiers. The raised left arm and the eyes turned towards the viewer cause it to resemble the Hagiosoritissa (or Chalkopratissa) Virgin, an ancient

icon in the Chalkoprateia Church in Constantinople. As far as Tver icon-painting is concerned, this iconography could have come via the Balkans (Mount Athos) as early as the end of the fourteenth century.

Provenance: From the Church of Obodovo village near Torzhok. Acquired by the Rublev Museum in 1966. Along with the other icons in the Deesis tier could have reached the village church from the Torzhok Monastery of the Nativity, which possessed the village in the sixteenth and seventeenth centuries, or from the older Monastery of SS Boris and Gleb to which the Nativity Monastery became attached in 1690.

Exhibitions: 1968 Moscow; 1969—70 Moscow; 1972 Moscow

References: Tver Painting 1970, p. 19 (No. 8); Popov 1970, p. 318, note 29; Vagner, Kukles, Tikhomirova 1972, p. 94, ill. 2; Yevseyeva, Kochetkov, Sergeyev 1974, p. 21, pl. 15; Idem 1983, pp. 17, 18, pls. 14, 15; * A. A. Saltykov, "Deesis Icons from the Village of Obodovo", in: *Early Russian Art. Problems and Attributions*, Moscow, 1977, pp. 188—198, ills. pp. 189, 191; Popov 1978, p. 191; Gusarova 1979, pp. 111—113, 125; Popov 1979, p. 110ff, 275—278, ills. pp. 129, 384, 385; Saltykov 1981, pp. 14, 243, ills. 15, 16, 21, 22

18, 19. ST JOHN THE BAPTIST
From a half-length Deesis tier. First half of the 15th century
80.5×57.5
Rublev Museum of Early Russian Art, Moscow
Inv. No КП 442

State of preservation: Similar to Cat. Nos. 16, 17.

Iconography: See Cat. Nos. 16, 17. The presentation here is more traditional, although variants are known in fourteenth-century icon-painting analogous with the *Virgin* icon of this tier.

Provenance: See Cat. Nos. 16, 17.

Exhibitions: See Cat. Nos. 16, 17.

References: K. Wessel, "Johannes Baptisten (Prodromos)", in: *Reallexikon*, 1975—1976, vol. III, issue 20—21, col. 616—647; * O. S. Popova, "The

Icon of *St John the Precursor* of the Mid-14th Century from the Hermitage", in: *The Art of Western Europe and Byzantium*, Moscow, 1978; Further see Cat. Nos. 16, 17.

20—22. THE NATIVITY OF THE VIRGIN
First half of the 15th century. Tver
32×24
Russian Museum, St Petersburg
Inv. No. ДРЖ 2131

State of preservation: Good on the whole. Much crackling over the entire surface with glazings and gilding partially eroded by whiting. The repoussé silver mount is of the sixteenth century.

Iconography: A simplified abbreviated version of the scene which lacks the figure of St Joachim and also the table, an ever-present attribute of the episode in fourteenth- and fifteenth-century icon- and wall-painting. The treatment of the subject has parallels in early works going back to the eleventh century and also among individual examples of Western fourteenth-century icons and book illuminations associated with what is known as the *maniera greca* (noted by Lafontaine-Dosogne, see Cat. No. 15).

Provenance: From the Suzdal Convent of the Intercession of the Virgin, presumably originally donated by someone from Tver. In the late sixteenth century it was to be found among the convent's smaller (*piad*) icons. Acquired by the Russian Museum in 1914.

Exhibitions: 1967 Moscow, Tretyakov Gallery

References: * *Report of the Alexander III Russian Museum for 1914*, Petro-

grad, 1915, p. 22; Grabar 1926, pp. 16, 195; Idem 1966, pp. 39, 157; * V. Georgievsky, *Works of Old Russian Art in the Suzdal Museum*, Moscow, 1927. Supplement 1. *Inventory of the Suzdal Convent of the Intercession of the Virgin for 7105/1597*, p. 34; Dmitriyev 1940, p. 35; Russian Museum. Guide 1954, p. 17, ill. 147; Voronin, Lazarev 1955, pp. 10, 12, ill. p. 13; USSR. Old Russian Icons 1958, ill. p. 15; * A. N. Ovchinnikov, "Concerning the Question of Vladimir-Suzdalian 15th-Century Painting (the 15th-Century Icon of the *Intercession of the Virgin* from the Vladimir-Suzdal Museum)", in: *Restored Masterpieces*, Moscow, 1963, p. 20; Lafontaine-Dosogne 1964, I, pp. 50, 115, 116; Rostov-Suzdalian Painting 1967, No. 68, pp. 99, 100; * G. Vzdornov, "On North-Eastern Russian Painting of the 12th—15th Centuries", *Iskusstvo* (Art), 1969, No. 10, pp. 60, 62; Vzdornov 1970, p. 356, ill. p. 357; * N. Golizovsky, "About Suzdalian Painting", in: *Treasures of Suzdal*, compiled by S. Yamshchikov, Moscow, 1970, p. 107; Popov 1970, p. 351; Rozanova 1970, No. 48; Popov 1979, pp. 134, 135, 279—281, ills. pp. 386, 387; Lazarev 1983, pp. 129, 501 (No. 134)

23. THE METROPOLITAN PETER
From a half-length Deesis tier. First half of the 15th century

158×96
Tretyakov Gallery, Moscow
Inv. No. 19773

State of preservation: Uneven. The upper part with the face, headdress and omophorion on the saint's shoulders is in a better state of preservation. Considerable losses of priming down to the panel itself in the lower half. Crackling and abrasion of the paint layer with the glazing and background gilding partially erased. Visible cracks along the joints of the panel boards.

Iconography: The Metropolitan Peter (in office 1308—26) whose feast-days are December 21/January 3 and August 24/September 6 was the first Metropolitan of Kiev and All-Russia to take up residence in Moscow. The oldest full-length depiction of him can be found together with portrayals of other Metropolitans who were particularly revered in Muscovy, such as Maximus Theognostus and Alexius, on a 1389/90 pall now in the

Historical Museum, Moscow, which was commissioned by Maria of Tver, wife of Simeon the Proud, Grand Prince of Moscow. The second oldest depiction occurs on the so-called Lesser Sakkos of the Metropolitan Photius in the Armoury, which dates from the turn of the fifteenth century coinciding with his period in office (1408/10—31).

No earlier painted portrayals of the Metropolitan that could be compared with our icon are known, in particular there is no clarity over the date of the now lost icons depicting Russian Metropolitans that comprised part of the Deesis tier produced by the Rublev circle in the Vladimir Cathedral of the Dormition (after 1408). From the late fifteenth century, incorporation of Moscow's first Metropolitan in Deesis tiers became a stable tradition. The iconographic type here is of the kind usual for Deesis tiers (see Cat. Nos. 16, 17; 18, 19). The Kremlin Armoury possesses an embroidered sakkos or dalmatic which belonged to the Metropolitan Peter, dated 1322. Picked out in needlework on its sky-blue satin are four-pointed gold crosses enclosed in medallions separated by vertical stripes. The garments depicted on the icon accord to some degree with the Metropolitan's actual vestments: however, the colours are far richer.

Provenance: It has been suggested that this icon originally came from Tver's oldest, Otroch, Monastery where it was displayed in the refectory. According to documentary evidence from the Tver archives, in 1927 it entered the Central Restoration Workshops from which it was subsequently transferred to the Tretyakov Gallery in 1934. In all likelihood the cult of the Moscow Metropolitan infiltrated anti-Muscovite Tver due to the activities of Bishop Arsenius of Tver (1390—1409), a close associate of Metropolitan Cyprian, who saw himself as Peter's successor in the effort to integrate and consolidate the Russian Orthodox Church (* L. A. Dmitriyev, "The Role and Significance of the Metropolitan Cyprian in the History of Old Russian Literature", in: *Papers of the Department of Old Russian Literature*, Moscow—Leningrad, 1963, vol. 19, pp. 236—254). It is quite possible that the icon could date from the first third of the fifteenth century.

Exhibitions: 1960 Moscow; 1969—70 Moscow; 1976 Leningrad

References: Rublev Exhibition 1960, p. 41 (No. 74); Antonova, Mneva 1963, 1, No. 200 (p. 235); Tver Painting 1970, p. 20 (No. 11); Popov 1970, pp. 336, 338, ill. p. 337; Yevseyeva, Kochétkov, Sergeyev 1974, pp. 26, 27, pls. 24, 25; Idem 1983, pp. 21, 22; Gusarova 1979, pp. 109, 111, 122; Plugin 1974, p. 106; Popov 1979, pp. 11, 141—145, 174, 276, 286, 290, 296, ill. p. 143; Dionysius 1981, p. 25 (No. 2); * E. S. Smirnova, *Moscow Icons: 14th and 15th Centuries*, Leningrad, 1988, pp. 30, 284, Cat. Nos. 117, 119

24. THE VIRGIN HODEGETRIA
First half or middle of the 15th century

30×23

Museum of History and Art, Sergiyev Posad

Inv. No. 5002

State of preservation: Good. Main losses due to repeated change or reworking of mountings. Minor later fillings of priming on the Virgin's garments and Christ's head and neck. Much crackling. The repoussé silver covering of the background is the fifteenth — sixteenth century and of the margins, the sixteenth century.

Iconography: Traditional and closest to fifteenth-century Muscovite icons, a version, which after the making of a copy of a Smolensk icon, commissioned in 1456 by Grand Prince Vasily II, came to be known as the *Smolensk Hodegetria* (see also Cat. Nos. 12—14).

Provenance: Prior to its acquisition by the Zagorsk (Sergiyev Museum) in 1920, it was in the sacristy of the Trinity-St Sergius Monastery. Still earlier it had been in the so-called *piad* (small-icon) tier of one of the Monastery's churches, as is indicated by an inscription and number on the reverse. Another inscription, stating in Russian, "of the Princess Anna Mikulinskaya", is from the sixteenth century and connects the icon with the princely family of the Mikulinsky appanage. Two Annas are known: one was the daughter of the Muscovite boyar Fiodor Koshka who married Mikhail Alexandrovich Mikulinsky in the first half of the fifteenth century, the other was married to Vasily Andreyevich Mikulinsky a century later; in 1540 she owned the village of Vasilyevskoye from which several Tver icons derive (Cat. Nos. 12—14; 15).

Exhibitions: 1921, Sergiyev; 1969—70 Moscow

References: Olsufyev 1920, pp. 80—82

(No. 11/393), 226; * Yu. A. Olsufyev, *Parallelism and Concentricity in the Ancient Icon as Indications of Diataxis*, Sergiyev, 1927, pp. 8—11, figs. 1—3; * Yu. A. Olsufyev, *The Structure of Highlighting. A Historical and Iconological Study of Works of Art in the Collection of the Former Trinity-S. Sergius Monastery*, Sergiyev, 1928 pp. 14, 31 (note 16), fig. 7; Olsufyev 1936, p. 44; J. A. Lebedewa, *Andrej Rubljow und seine Zeitgenossen*, Dresden, 1962, p. 30, ill. 10; * O. A. Belobrova, "14th-Century Painting", in:

The Trinity-St Sergius Monastery. Art Relics, Moscow, 1968, p. 76, pl. 65; Nikolayeva 1969, p. 28, pl. 3; Tver Painting 1970, p. 18 (No. 7); Popov 1970, p. 339; Popov 1973, p. 65; Yevseyeva, Kochetkov, Sergeyev 1974, p. 24, pl. 23; Idem 1983, p. 21; Nikolayeva 1977, pp. 29, 30, No. 100 (pp. 74, 75); Popov 1979, pp. 130, 131ff, 281—283, ill. p. 388

25, 26. ROYAL DOORS. LEFT LEAF: ST JOHN CHRYSOSTOM. RIGHT LEAF: ST BASIL THE GREAT
First half of the 15th century

111.5×35 (each leaf)
Tretyakov Gallery, Moscow
Inv. No. 12002 (left-hand leaf) and
Inv. No. 29560 (right-hand leaf)

State of preservation: The upper part of the leaves which featured a scene of the Annunciation has been lost. There are also considerable losses of the panel and priming below. Likewise minor losses and abrasions of the paint layer, which have been touched up with tempera and linseed varnish. The gilding of the haloes is of later, sixteenth- or seventeenth-century origin.

Iconography: Of the several designs employed in Russian painting in the thirteenth — sixteenth centuries to embellish Royal or Holy Doors, two were very popular — depictions of the Evangelists and depictions of Church Fathers, more often than not St Basil the Great and John Chrysostom, the creators of the Liturgies. On the earliest doors the figures of these two saints are shown full-face. Later they were presented three-quarter-face as on these Royal Doors from Tver. Nevertheless this work is somewhat archaic for the time, since fifteenth-century Doors usually depicted the Evangelists (A. Grabar, "Deux notes sur l'histoire de l'iconostase d'après des monuments de Yougoslavie", *Transactions of the Institute of Byzantine Studies*, 7, Belgrade, 1961, pp. 13—17; Djorović — Lubincović 1965). The text on the scrolls held by the two saints paraphrases the Eucharistic prayer from the Liturgy of St Basil the Great.

Provenance: From the 1671 wooden Church of the Entry into Jerusalem of the Nektaryev parish, formerly the Nektaryev Convent of the Intercession

of the Virgin, near Tver. The left-hand leaf was acquired by the painter I. S. Ostroukhov. The right-hand leaf entered the Tver Museum as early as 1878. The left-hand leaf was transferred to the Tretyakov Gallery from the Ostroukhov Museum in 1929. The right-hand leaf was sent to the Central Restoration Workshops in Moscow for renovation. After the 1929—32 exhibition it was transferred to the Russian Museum from which it entered the Tretyakov Gallery in 1933. The Nektaryev parish owes its name to Nektarii, the founder of the convent. There is no reliable information about him but he is believed to have lived in the late fourteenth and the first decades of the fifteenth centuries (* *The Tver Patericon*, Kazan, 1907, pp. 59, 60)

Exhibitions: 1913 Moscow; 1929—32 Germany, England, Austria, USA; 1969—70 Moscow

References: Zhiznevsky 1889, pp. 45, 47 (No. 60); * *Exhibition of Early Russian Art at the Imperial Moscow Institute of Archaeology. Catalogue*, Moscow, 1913, section 1, No. 21, ill. p. 12; * P. Muratov, *Early Russian Painting in the I. S. Ostroukhov Collection*, Moscow, 1914, pp. 12, 13, ill. p. 12; * N. Punin, "Hellenism and the East in Icon-Painting: The Icon Collections of I. S. Ostroukhov and S. P. Riabushinsky", in: *Russkaya Ikona* (The Russian Icon), 1914, No. 3, p. 184, ill. p. 185; * L. Matsulevich, "Fragments of Wall-Painting in the Snetogorsk Monastery", *Transactions of the Department of Russian and Slavonic Archaeology of the Imperial Russian Society of Archaeology*, St Petersburg, 1915, issue 10, p. 35; O. Wulf, M. Alpatoff, *Denkmäler der Ikonenmalerei*, Dresden, 1925, pp. 266, 267, ill. 34; * A. Anisimov, "The Pre-Mongol Period of Early Russian Painting", *Voprosy restavratsii* (Problems of Restoration), Moscow,

1928, issue 2, p. 143;
* A. I. Anisimov, *Early Russian Art. A Collection of Articles*, Moscow 1983, p. 316; * G. V. Zhidkov, *Mid-14th-Century Moscow Painting*, Moscow, 1928, pp. 121, 141 (note 323); Ancient Russian Icons 1929, No. 9; Denkmäler altrussischer Malerei 1929, No. 9; Ph. Schweinfurth 1930, p. 243, ill. 85; Catalogue of Russian Icons 1931, No. 9; D. Ainaloff, *Geschichte der russischen Monumentalkunst zur Zeit des Grossfürstentums Moskau*, Berlin — Leipzig, 1933, pp. 89, 90, pl. 45a; Olsufyev 1936, p. 47; Nekrasov 1937, p. 132, fig. 79; Voronin, Lazarev 1955, p. 30, ill.

p. 29; Antonova, Mneva 1963, I, No. 199 (pp. 233—235, pls. 138, 139); Lazarev 1965, p. 70; Djorović-Lubincović 1965, p. 32, ill. 26; Tver Painting 1970, pp. 17, 18 (No. 6); Popov 1970, pp. 317, 320, 322; Yevseyeva, Kochetkov, Sergeyev 1974, p. 18, pls. 10, 11; Idem 1983, p. 15; Smirnova 1976, pp. 167—169; Popov 1978, p. 190, ill. p. 189; Popov 1979, pp. 68—77, 265—268, ills. pp. 71, 378, 379; Smirnova, Laurina, Gordiyenko 1982, pp. 337, 340; Lazarev 1983, pp. 130, 503 (No. 142)

27—33. CHRIST IN MAJESTY
From a Deesis tier. Second quarter or middle of the 15th century

209×137
Russian Museum, St Petersburg
Inv. No. 1958

State of preservation: Uneven, with the paint layer heavily abraded in places. Particular damage was done during renovations in the late nineteenth century and early twentieth century (on most other icons from the same tier in the possession of the same museum the original painting is virtually non-existent; see Cat. Nos. 34, 35; 36, 37). As far as can be judged, the first major repairs of the entire tier were undertaken in the sixteenth century when it was still in Tver. The next renovation was carried out after the icons had already been transferred to Kashin: in January 1667 the well-known Armoury painter Ivan Filatov or Filatyev was sent there "on the tsar's business" (* A. I. Uspensky, *Tsarist Icon-Painters and Painters of the 17th Century. A Glossary*, Moscow, 1910, p. 283).

Iconography: The main source for this very special symbolical image of the enthroned Christ were the texts of the visions of the Prophet Ezekiel and the Revelation (see Cat. Nos. 16, 17; for the symbolism of the throne. Th. Bogyay, "Hetoimasia", in: *Reallexikon*, 1971, vol. II, issue 16, col. 1189—1202). The Gospel text was interpreted in fifteenth- and sixteenth-century Russian works in two different main versions: this icon is closer to the Muscovite variant (cf: John VII, 24; Matthew VII, 2; see Plugin 1974, pp. 86—101). In the corner of the sphere are the emblems of the Evangelists, while the fiery wheel-shaped

forces at Christ's feet are part of the heavenly host.

Provenance: The icons of the Deesis (see also Cat. Nos. 34—37) and the Prophets (Cat. Nos. 63—68) tiers entered the Russian Museum in 1940 from the Kashin Museum of Local Lore to which they had earlier been transferred from the town's Cathedral of the Resurrection. This cathedral had in turn acquired the works from Tver's Cathedral of the Transfiguration. Their presence there together with the Church Feasts icons (Cat. Nos. 38—62) is recorded in the inventory for 1626. The view has been voiced (Golubev 1979, p. 368) that this group of icons was produced after the fire in Tver in 1449; however, it is quite possible that they were brought to the Cathedral of the Transfiguration from another major church in Tver built during the reign of the Grand Prince Boris Alexandrovich, for instance, the Church of SS Boris and Gleb (1433—38), or the Cathedral of the Archangel Michael (1452—55). This second version is supported above all by a report of the fire that occurred in Tver on July 22, 1537, in which the interior decoration of the ancient Cathedral of the Transfiguration was reduced to ashes (* *The Complete Collection of Russian Chronicles*, St Petersburg, 1853, vol. 6, p. 302; * *The Writings of the Very Reverend Maxim the Greek in Their Russian Translation*, Trinity-St Sergius Monastery, 1910, part 1, chapter XX, pp. 164—174). Within a short period the interior of this late thirteenth-century cathedral was renovated with "all Holy images" painted, as Maxim the Greek puts it, by "skilful artists with precious adornment of gold and silver" (*Ibid.*, chapter XII, pp. 183—185).

It is more than likely that for this purpose older icons were used from one of the above-mentioned churches in the former princely court (the chronicles do not say whether it burned down or not: there are no traces of fire on the icons in the tier; Cat. Nos. 27—68).

Apart from the icons presented here, the Russian Museum possesses another eight icons from the Deesis tier, namely the *Virgin*, *St John the Baptist*, the *Apostle Peter*, the *Apostle Paul*, *St John Chrysostom*, *St Basil the Great*, *St George* and *St Demetrius of Thessalonica*, in which the original painting is virtually lost. Though the 1626 Inventory gives the same number of icons, eleven, this cannot have been the original number since the total width of the fourteen icons of Church Feasts mentioned in the inventory does not correspond to the indicated number of icons in the Deesis tier. The dimensions would match, if we had fifteen icons in the Deesis tier and eighteen in the Church Feasts tier (around 14.80 metres). This is the same number as in the iconostasis of the Trinity Cathedral at the Trinity-St Sergius Monastery which was painted by artists of the Rublev circle in 1425—27, i.e. fifteen icons for the Deesis tier and another nineteen for the Church Feasts tier. These icons are the nearest surviving contemporaries of those from Tver. In the next, Prophets, tier of the Trinity Cathedral iconostasis we find thirteen half-length figures, or two on each icon. The Tver iconostasis may have had the same number of tiers and a corresponding number of icons. The Prophets tier was located beneath the vaulting of a relatively small church (which was nevertheless larger than the Cathedral of the Transfiguration) and was smaller than the others. Thus it is evident that the ensemble had suffered significant losses prior to 1626. Only half of the Church Feasts icons mentioned in the inventory are now extant. The icons of the Deesis and Prophets tiers were transferred to Kashin, in all likelihood after the old Cathedral in Tver was rebuilt in 1634—35. (See also Cat. Nos. 38—43.)

Exhibitions: 1920 Moscow; 1976 Leningrad

References (presented is a summary list including exhibition catalogues, since in most publications an appraisal of the individual icons is combined with an overall appreciation):
* *Tver Eparchy Gazette*, 1885, No. 8, pp. 259, 260 (*Ibid.*, 1897, No. 22, p. 785); * I. Zavyalov, *Materials for the History and Archaeology of the Town of Kashin*, Tver, 1901, p. 6; * I. Zavyalov, *The Town of Kashin, Its History, Shrines and Sights*, St Petersburg, 1909, pp. 19—24; * A. I. Uspensky, *Tsarist Icon-Painters and Painters of the 17th Century*, Moscow, 1916, vol. 4, pls. XXXVI—XXXIX; * N. D. Protasov, "Kashin Monuments", *Transactions of the Russian Academy of the History of Material Culture*, Petrograd, vol. 1, 1921; Grabar 1926, p. 107; Idem 1966, pp. 200—208; Ancient Russian Icons 1929, Nos. 39, 40; Denkmäler altrussischer Malerei 1929, p. 15, Nos. 36, 37; *Masterpieces of Russian Painting*, London, 1930, pp. 46, 113, 116, pls. XVIII, XXXI, XXXV; Schweinfurth 1930, p. 326, ill. 128; Catalogue of Russian Icons 1931, Nos. 39, 40; Olsufyev 1935, p. 32, fig. 12; Dmitriyev 1940, p. 35, ill. p. 37; * Yu. Dmitriyev, "Kashin Art Relics", *Reports of the Russian Museum*, 11/1947, Leningrad, 1948; J. Myslivec, *Icona*, Prague, 1947, p. 25; Russian Museum. Guide 1954, p. 22; Voronin, Lazarev 1955, pp. 32—36, ills. pp. 35, 37, 39; Malarstwo rosyiskie XIV—XX w. 1957, No. 10; Yagodovskaya 1958, p. 49; *Russian Painting from the 13th to the 20th Century. Catalogue*, London, 1959, No. 8; * N. E. Mneva, A. B. Zernova, "Cleaning of Monuments of Old Russian Easel Tempera Painting", in: *Cultural Monuments. Studies and Restoration*, Moscow, 1960, issue 2, p. 184; Onasch 1961, pl. 114; Antonova, Mneva 1963, 1, Nos. 206, 207 (pp. 240—242, pls. 149—151); Grabar 1966, pp. 242, 243, 245; * M. V. Alpatov, *Studies of the History of Russian Art*, Moscow, vol. 1, 1967, pp. 172, 173, ill. 122; L'art russe des Scythes à nos jours 1967, No. 268; Sixth Exhibition 1969, p. 87; * S. Yamshchikov, *Old Russian Painting. New Discoveries*, Leningrad, 1969, pl. 31; * N. A. Gagman, "The Principles of Restoring Losses in Old Russian Easel Paintings", in: *The All-Union Conference on the Theoretical Principles of Restoring Old Russian Easel Painting*, Moscow, 1970, pp. 157, 158, figs. 57, 58; Tver Painting 1970, pp. 28, 29 (Nos. 24, 25); * M. V. Alpatov, *Treasures of Russian Art. 11th—16th Centuries (Painting)*, Leningrad, 1970, p. 282, pls. 162, 163; Popov 1971, pp. 106, 107; Popov 1973, pp. 127, 128; * M. V. Alpatov, *The Colours of Old Russian Painting*, Moscow, 1974, p. 15, pl. 63; Yevseyeva, Kochetkov, Sergeyev 1974, pp. 42—45, pls. 56—69; Idem 1983, pp. 25—28, pls. 40—52; * Yu. G. Bobrov, "The History of the Development of the Theory and Practice of Restoring Old Russian Easel

Paintings. The Russian Museum 1910—41", in: *Problems of the Development of Russian Art*, Leningrad, 1976, issue 8, pp. 15, 16; * E. K. Guseva, "The Icon of the Virgin of the Sign from the Kashin Deesis Tier", in: *Old Russian Art. Problems and Attributions*, Moscow, 1977; Popov 1978, pp. 223—252; Popov 1979, pp. 150—172, 290—304, ills. pp. 151, 153, 155, 157, 159, 163, 164, 167, 169, 171, 404—432; Golubev 1979, pp. 366—368; Ryndina 1979, pp. 495, 549, 569, ills. pp. 595, 596; Dionysius 1981, pp. 26—28 (Nos. 5—7), ills. 1—9; Smirnova, Laurina, Gordiyenko 1982, pp. 216, 223, 232, 250, 313, 314, 326, 327; Lazarev 1983, pp. 131, 503 (No. 141); * *Restoration of Museum Treasures in the USSR. An Exhibition Catalogue*, I, Moscow, 1985, pp. 57 (ill. 95), 93

34, 35. THE ARCHANGEL MICHAEL
From a Deesis tier. Second quarter or middle of the 15th century

210×96
Russian Museum, St Petersburg
Inv. No. 2111

State of preservation: Original painting damaged in places during renovations. Wherever losses are greatest (in the folds of the garments, fragments of the wings, shadows on the face and locks of hair), restorers retained some overpainting.

Iconography: The pose and contour of the figure are traditional for Deesis compositions from the fourteenth and fifteenth centuries. The sceptre held in the right hand is the emblem of the divine messenger. The transparent orb with Christ's monogram held in the left hand is emblematical of the Lord's command. A cryptographic inscription runs along the fringe of the cloak (cf. Cat. No. 24; for the composition of Deesis tiers see also Cat. Nos. 16, 17; for the most comprehensive enumeration of the various ways of portraying angels and archangels see D. I. Pallas, "Himmelsmächte, Erzengel und Engel", in: *Reallexikon*, 1972, vol. III, issue 17, col. 13—119; and for the different ways of presenting the orb see A. Grabar, *L'iconoclasme byzantin*, Paris, 1957, pp. 219—222 and K. Wessel, "Glorie", in: *Reallexikon* 1971, vol. IV, issue 14, col. 867—882).

Provenance: See Cat. Nos. 27—33.
Exhibitions: 1976 Leningrad
References: See Cat. Nos. 27—33.

36, 37. THE ARCHANGEL GABRIEL
From a Deesis tier. Second quarter or middle of the 15th century

210×97
Russian Museum, St Petersburg
Inv. No. 1955

State of preservation: Similar to Cat. Nos. 27—33; 34, 35. All traces of additions made during earlier restorations have been removed from the original painting.

Iconography: See Cat. Nos. 34, 35.
Provenance: See Cat. Nos. 27—33.
Exhibitions: See Cat. Nos. 27—33.
References: See Cat. Nos. 27—33.

38—43. THE NATIVITY OF CHRIST
From a Church Feasts tier. Second quarter or middle of the 15th century

103×81
Tretyakov Gallery, Moscow
Inv. No. 17297

State of preservation: Uneven. Glazings eroded in places. Greatest damage done to the ground and margins in the lower part in which there are major insertions of later priming. Earlier re-painting left during the restoration of losses, with the greatest losses touched up.

Iconography: The subject is based on the Gospel text (Matthew II, 1—12 and Luke II, 6—20) and also on the

Protevangelium of St James the Less. The composition adheres to the traditional fifteenth-century style of Russian painting, which in turn derives from the variant established in fourteenth-century Paleologue art (Lexikon 1970, vol. 2, col. 86—120; Lafontaine-Dosogne 1975, pp. 208—214). The rightward turn of the Virgin's couch and the Magi on horseback are parallelled in contemporary and later Muscovite icon-painting. A different variant was dominant in Novgorodian art (Smirnova, Laurina, Gordiyenko 1982, pp. 232, 233). Initially the Church Feasts tier, incorporating this and other icons (Cat. Nos. 44—62) was much larger apparently approximating the composition of the 1425—27 iconostasis of the Trinity Cathedral of the Trinity-St Sergius Monastery (see Cat. Nos. 27—33).

Provenance: Similar to the icons from the Deesis (Cat. Nos. 27—37) and Prophets (Cat. Nos. 63—68) tiers. At one time the Church Feasts icons had adorned the Tver Cathedral of the Transfiguration. However, unlike the icons of the Deesis and Prophets tiers, which were transferred to Kashin, apparently after the rebuilding of the Cathedral in 1634—35, it is not clear what happened to the Church Feasts icons. At any rate at the beginning of the twentieth century all seven icons presented here were in the Tver Church of St Nicholas-on-the-Menagerie. In 1927 they entered the Tver Museum and subsequently found their way to the Central Restoration Workshops, but after the 1929—32 exhibitions some were transferred to the Tretyakov Gallery, others to the Russian Museum in 1934.

Exhibitions: 1929—32 Germany, England, Austria, USA; 1959 London; 1967—68 Paris; 1969—70 Moscow

References: See Cat. Nos. 27—33.

44—48. THE PRESENTATION IN THE TEMPLE

From a Church Feasts tier. Second quarter or middle of the 15th century
103×81
Russian Museum, St Petersburg
Inv. No. 2132

State of preservation: Good on the whole with considerable insertions of new priming in the margins and the lower part of the icon and numerous traces of nails from the mounting.

Iconography: The Gospels (Luke II, 21—38; feast-day 2/15 February) do not directly indicate where this incident took place. In fourteenth- and fifteenth-century painting there are two dominant variants. In one the scene is set in front of the Temple of Jerusalem and the composition is asymmetrical with a sense of space that is distinctly associated with the early Paleologue tradition. In the second version the scene is set in front of the sanctuary and the composition is strictly centralized. The version presented in this icon derives from a late fourteenth-century fresco in the Novgorod Church of the Dormition-on-the-Volotovo-Field and is to be seen in a Novogorodian icon of the second half of the fifteenth century. The second variant is more common in fifteenth-century Russian icon-painting (Smirnova, Laurina, Gordiyenko 1982, pp. 216, 250, 251).

Provenance: See Cat. Nos. 38—43.

Exhibitions: 1929—32 Germany, England, Austria, USA; 1976 Leningrad

References: See Cat. Nos. 27—33.

49—52. THE RAISING OF LAZARUS

From a Church Feasts tier. Second quarter or middle of the 15th century

103×81
Russian Museum, St Petersburg
Inv. No. 2723

State of preservation: Similar to Cat. Nos. 38—43 but somewhat better.

Iconography: In accordance with the Gospels (John XI, 1—45; movable feasts on the Saturday before Palm Sunday and during the Eighteenth Week after Pentecost). The sources of the compositional arrangement are similar to the other Church Feasts icons of this group. The scene is in its way the sum of several variants with the spatial and dynamic effect heightened. There are no known direct parallels in Russian painting of the late fourteenth and fifteenth centuries (for greater detail see Pokrovsky 1892, pp. 249—257; K. Wessel, "Erweckung des Lazarus", in: *Reallexikon*, 1968, vol. II, issue 11, col. 396—414; Plugin 1974, pp. 57—79).

Provenance: See Cat. Nos. 38—43.

Exhibitions: See Cat. Nos. 44—48.

References: See Cat. Nos. 27—33.

53—55. THE ENTRY INTO JERUSALEM
From a Church Feasts tier. Second quarter or middle of the 15th century
61×84
Tretyakov Gallery, Moscow
Inv. No. 20693

State of preservation: Patchy. Part of the panel and priming in the lower half were added much later while the original margins have been chiselled away. The painting was filled-in in the nineteenth century. The original paint layer has been damaged in places in the upper part and there are losses of the glazings (the 1626 Inventory explains that "the image of the Entry into Jerusalem mounting was struck by lightning". Subsequently this led to the losses indicated and to repeated renovations).

Iconography: In accordance with the Gospels (Matthew XXI, 8—11; Mark XI, 7—11; Luke XIX, 28—44 and John XII, 12—18. The movable feast is in the Sixth Week of Lent, one week before Easter). Judging by the extant fragments, the compositional type is traditional for fifteenth-century painting. The panoramic view of Jerusalem has analogies in Muscovite icon-painting of the first third of the same century: see Cat. Nos. 89, 90 (for greater detail see Pokrovsky 1892, pp. 258—264; E. L. Palli, "Einzug in Jerusalem", in: *Reallexikon*, 1967, vol. II, issue 9, col. 22—30 and also Cat. Nos. 89, 90).

Provenance: See Cat. Nos. 38—43.

Exhibitions: 1969—70 Moscow

References: See Cat. Nos. 27—33.

56, 57. THE BAPTISM OF CHRIST
From a Church Feasts tier. Second quarter or middle of the 15th century
103×80
Russian Museum, St Petersburg
Inv. No. 1891

State of preservation: Considerable losses of priming and abrasion of the paint layer. All subsequent additions have been removed during restoration; minor touchings up.

Iconography: In accordance with the Gospels (Matthew III, 13—17; Mark I, 9—11; Luke III, 21, 22; feast-day January 6/19). Typologically linked with Paleologue sources and on the whole corresponds to variants common in fifteenth-century Russian painting. Unlike early icons of the Balkan circle and those of Muscovite and Novgorodian provenance, there is no personification of the River Jordan and the Sea (for the iconography see * F. I. Schmit, "An Iconographic Variant of the Baptism of the Saviour", *Transactions of the Russian Archeological Institute in Constantinople*, Sofia, 1911, issue 15; M. Tatić-Djurić, "The Icon of the Baptism of Christ", *Collection of Articles of the National Museum*, vol. 4, Belgrade, 1964; Lexikon 1972, vol. 4, col. 247—255).

Provenance: See Cat. Nos. 38—43. Most likely the artist was an apprentice of the chief painter of the ensemble.

Exhibitions: 1976 Leningrad; 1983 Moscow

References: See Cat. Nos. 27—33.

58—60. THE ASCENSION
From a Church Feasts tier. Second quarter or middle of the 15th century
102×81
Tretyakov Gallery, Moscow
Inv. No. 22039

State of preservation: Similar to Cat. Nos. 38—43. Touching up of abrasions and losses of the paint layer with later additions surviving in places.

Iconography: In accordance with the text of the Acts of the Apostles (1, 9—

11; the movable feast on the Thursday of the Sixth Week after Easter). Like most Church Feasts icons in the tier it derives from earlier prototypes. Unlike fifteenth-century Muscovite icons the figure of the Virgin is presented three-quarter-face, while the poses of the Apostles are full of vigour (*S. A. Zhelebov, "Iconographic Schemes of the Ascension of Christ and the Sources of Their Origin", *A Collection of Articles Devoted to the Memory of N. P. Kondakov*, Prague, 1026).

Provenance: See Cat. Nos. 38—43. The artist has a distinctive manner and may have also produced the icon of the *Descent of the Holy Ghost* (Cat.

Nos. 61, 62). However, due to the poor degree of preservation it is difficult to identify which icons of the Prophets tier he may have painted.

Exhibitions: See Cat. Nos. 38—43.
References: See Cat. Nos. 27—33.

61, 62. THE DESCENT OF THE HOLY GHOST
From a Church Feasts tier. Second quarter or middle of the 15th century
103×81
Tretyakov Gallery, Moscow
Inv. No. 22058

State of preservation: Similar to Cat. Nos. 38—43; 58—60.

Iconography: Corresponds to the text of the Acts of the Apostles (I, 5, 8; II, 2—4; the movable feast on the 50th day after Easter whence the alternative title of *Pentecost*). In keeping with fourteenth- and fifteenth-century traditions (Smirnova, Laurina, Gordiyenko 1982, pp. 189, 190).

Provenance: See Cat. Nos. 38—43.
Exhibitions: See Cat. Nos. 38—43.
References: See Cat. Nos. 27—33.

63, 64. THE VIRGIN OF THE SIGN
From a Prophets tier. Second quarter or middle of the 15th century
133×100
Tretyakov Gallery, Moscow
Inv. No. 25541

State of preservation: Patchy. Considerable losses of priming and painting in the centre and along the upper and lower edges. The panel has been filled in at the top. The faces bear minor vestiges of overpainting.

Iconography: The theme of this central icon of the third, Prophets, tier of the iconostasis derives from some of the prophetic visions and pronouncements to be found in the Books of the Prophets (Moses, Isaiah, etc.) in the Old Testament. The association is confirmed by the composition of the tier which indicates a primary link between the Virgin of the Sign and the images of the Prophets. Yet separate depictions of the subject are also known, as is its presentation in combination with a diverse selection of figures. The theme was especially widespread in fifteenth-century Novgorodian icon-painting (* N. P. Kondakov, *The Iconography of the Mother of God*, Petrograd, 1915, vol. II, pp. 103—151; M. Tatić-Djurić, "The Icon of the Virgin of the Sign", *Zbornik za likovne umetnosti*, Novi Sad, 1977, No. 13). Later, in the fifteenth century, Prophets tiers were produced where the central image was a depiction of King David alone or with King Solomon (Smirnova, Laurina, Gordiyenko 1982, pp. 325—327). Half-length figures were the norm in this tier, while from the mid-sixteenth century there were also full-length figures. The choice of figures for the Prophets tier did not change substantially with time. However, in the early stages, prior to the appearance of the special Patriarchs tier with its central icon of the New Testament Trinity-Paternity in the middle or third quarter of the sixteenth century, one could not infrequently encounter images of the

Patriarchs Moses and Jacob in the composition of this tier (Cat. No. 68); the icon of Moses from the same tier, with later painting, is in the Russian Museum. For the possible original dimensions of the Prophets tier that included the icons presented, see Cat. Nos. 27—33.

Provenance: See Cat. Nos. 27—33. In 1919 the icon was sent to Moscow for restoration and in 1934 it was transferred to the Tretyakov Gallery. Apart from the icons from this tier that are presented below (Cat. Nos. 65—68), the Russian Museum owns four icons whose original painting was greatly damaged during renovations or is almost completely missing. The painter of this icon, as well as of Cat. Nos. 65—67, was the leading artist of the team which created the ensemble (Cat. Nos. 27—33).

Exhibitions: 1929—32 Germany, England, Austria, USA; 1969—70 Moscow; 1976 Leningrad

References: See Cat. Nos. 27—33.

65. KING DAVID
From a Prophets tier. Second quarter or middle of the 15th century
133×102
Russian Museum, St Petersburg
Inv. No. 1827

State of preservation: Largely similar to Cat. Nos. 63, 64. Losses of upper paint layers across almost the entire surface. Insertions and losses of priming partly touched up.

Iconography: According to the Bible David was Israel's second king after Saul and the Psalms are associated with his name. His representation as a warrior king, musician and poet was extremely common in medieval, including Russian, art. He was revered as prototype and direct ancestor of Christ (Matthew I, 1). The half-length figure of him on this icon is of a typology traditional of fifteenth-century icons in the Prophets tier. The text on the scroll reproduces the 44th psalm.

Provenance: See Cat. Nos. 27—33. In 1934 entered the Russian Museum from the Central Restoration Workshops.

Exhibitions: 1976 Leningrad

References: See Cat. Nos. 27—33.

66. KING SOLOMON
From a Prophets tier. Second quarter or middle of the 15th century
134×103
Russian Museum, St Petersburg
Inv. No. 1969

State of preservation: Similar to Cat. No. 65. During restoration later overpainting was retained in places. Considerable touching up.

Iconography: According to the Bible Solomon was the son and heir of King David. Many homilies and lyrical compositions are associated with him, especially the Parables and the Songs in the Old Testament. He is the hero of a plethora of apocryphal legends and ballads that were widely popular in old Russia (* A. N. Veselovsky, *Slavonic Legends about Solomon and Kitovras and Western Legends about Morolf and Merlin*, Petrograd, 1921; * A. V. Bagriy, "Concerning the Routes of the Dissemination of Legends about Solomon the Wise", in: *A Collection of Articles Honouring Academician A. I. Sobolevsky*, Leningrad, 1928). In the literature and art of the Christian world Solomon is esteemed as the ideal of the wise philosopher and mighty and magnificent king, who is presumed to have been familiar with the occult sciences, sundry architectural artifices and the like. As 'son of David', he is always portrayed as a beardless youth. The type of half-figure seen in this icon is traditional and characteristic of fifteenth-century Russian icon-painting. The text on the scroll paraphrases part of the Book of Proverbs (XXXI, 29).

Provenance: See Cat. Nos. 27—33. In 1940 entered the Russian Museum from the Kashin Museum of Local Lore.

Exhibitions: 1967 Moscow; 1969—70 Moscow

References: See Cat. Nos. 27—33.

67. THE PROPHET EZEKIEL
From a Prophets tier. Second quarter or middle of the 15th century

132×102
Russian Museum, St Petersburg
Inv. No. 1971

State of preservation: Similar to Cat. Nos. 65; 66. When earlier overpainted was known as *Habakkuk*.

Iconography: In the Bible Ezekiel is one of the major Prophets of Israel, author of a book included in the Old Testament. The visions and prophecies found there underlay a number of symbolically complex artistic themes that were popular in the Middle Ages (*Christ in Majesty*, see Cat. Nos. 27—33). As Christianity interpreted Old Testament images primarily in a transcendental manner, Ezekiel is not infrequently portrayed with Christ appearing to him or holding the celestial gate of Paradise, a symbol of the Virgin (Ezekiel XLIV, 1, 2). The type of half-length figure presented is traditional. The text on the scroll reproduces the passage describing the vision of the gate.

Provenance: See Cat. Nos. 27—33; 63, 64.

Exhibitions: 1967 Moscow; 1969—70, Moscow; 1976 Leningrad

References: See Cat. Nos. 27—33.

68. THE PATRIARCH JACOB
From a Prophets tier. Second quarter or middle of the 15th century

133×102
Russian Museum, St Petersburg
Inv. No. 1970

State of preservation: Mostly similar to Cat. No. 66, with less filling in at restoration.

Iconography: According to the Bible Jacob was son of Isaac and Rebecca and grandson of Abraham (Genesis XXV, 26). Commonest in the visual arts of the Middle Ages are two subjects associated with his life, namely the ladder which he saw in a dream, and Jacob wrestling with the God-Angel (Genesis XXVIII, 12—17 and XXXII, 24—30). The type of half-length figure here is traditional. The scroll reproduces the description of the vision of the ladder.

Provenance: See Cat. Nos. 27—33; 63, 64. The artist has a distinctive manner and may also have painted the other two extant icons from the Church Feasts tier (Cat. Nos. 58—60; 61, 62).

Exhibitions: 1969—70 Moscow; 1976 Leningrad

References: See Cat. Nos. 27—33.

69—72. CHRIST IN MAJESTY
From a Deesis tier. 15th century

116×84
Tretyakov Gallery, Moscow
Inv. No. 15053

State of preservation: Similar to Cat. Nos. 73—86. Repeated repairs to the wooden panel. Minor losses and later insertions of priming in the margins and in the lower part, abrasions of the paint layer, strong crackling, greatest losses on the representation of the Gospel.

Iconography: See Cat. Nos. 27—33 and for the Deesis tier composition, Cat. Nos. 16, 17. The text on the book that Christ holds is from the so-called Novgorodian variant (cf. Cat. Nos. 27—33).

Provenance: Similar to Cat. Nos. 6, 7. From archive data, such as the 1920 Inventory in the Tver archives, we cautiously suggest that this icon, along with the others in the tier, is from the wooden Church of the Nativity in Tver's Coachmen's (Yamskaya) Quarter. In 1765 this church was taken apart and reassembled in the Monastery of St Demetrius in the vicinity of Tver; later in the eighteenth century it was replaced by a stone church (* D. I. Karmanov, *Collected Works on the History of the Tver Territory*, Tver, 1893, p. 126). The leaf of the Royal Doors dating from the second half of the fifteenth century (Cat. No. 105) is from the same church. Only from the seventeenth century is there some extant information about the Monastery of St Demetrius. A. Anisimov acquired the icons from this tier for his collection no later than 1929. The group of icons including the Royal Doors (Cat. Nos. 85, 86) were created by a group or 'artel' of artists with similar manner of working. The author of *Christ in Majesty* also produced the *Virgin* (Cat. Nos. 73, 74). Although the style of the two icons is greatly reminiscent of the first half of the fifteenth century, they may have been created later.

Exhibitions: 1958 Moscow; 1969—70 Moscow

References: Voronin, Lazarev 1955, p. 32; Antonova, Mneva 1963, 1, No. 203 (pp. 237, 238, pls. 142—146); Vzdornov 1970, p. 358; Tver Painting 1970, p. 22 (No. 14); Popov 1970, pp. 317, 324, ill. p. 319; Yevseyeva, Kochetkov, Sergeyev 1974, pp. 29—31, pls. 30—41; Idem 1983, pp. 23, 24, pls. 26—37; Popov 1979, pp. 135—140, 283—287, ills. pp. 137, 139, 389—397; Smirnova, Laurina, Gordiyenko 1982, pp. 195—321; Lazarev 1983, p. 130

73, 74. THE VIRGIN
From a Deesis tier. 15th century

115×47
Tretyakov Gallery, Moscow
Inv. No. 15055

State of preservation: Similar to Cat. Nos. 69—72. Later overpainting retained on priming insertions.

Iconography: The type and contour of the figure are traditional for fifteenth-century Deesis icons (see also Cat. Nos. 16, 17).

Provenance: See Cat. Nos. 69—72.

Exhibitions: See Cat. Nos. 69—72.

References: See Cat. Nos. 69—72.

75. ST JOHN THE BAPTIST
From a Deesis tier. 15th century

115×41
Tretyakov Gallery, Moscow
Inv. No. 15054

State of preservation: Similar to Cat. Nos. 69—72; 73, 74. Side margins and part of the upper and lower margins sawn off. Original painting well preserved.

Iconography: The representation of St John the Baptist, whether given full length or half length in Deesis or other compositions, can be clothed in various ways. One is the chiton and himation (Cat. Nos. 18, 19) according to ancient Greek tradition, in the other his garment stresses the ascetic sermonizing character of the Prophet. In the second variant the saint will invariably be wearing camel skin, leaving the arms and legs partly bare. This ascetic type is commonest in early-fifteenth-century Russian Deesis tiers. In this icon the pose and outline are traditional, the only distinctively individual features being the exaggerated size and emphasized folds of the garment.

Provenance: See Cat. Nos. 69—72. The painter is second to the leading artist of the group and in all likelihood he also created the icon of the *Apostle Peter* (Cat. Nos. 77, 78).

Exhibitions: See Cat. Nos. 69—72.

References: See Cat. Nos. 69—72.

76. THE APOSTLE PAUL
From a Deesis tier. 15th century

113×47
Tretyakov Gallery, Moscow
Inv. No. 15056

State of preservation: Similar to other icons in the group. Side margins sawn off.

Iconography: See Cat. Nos. 77, 78.

Provenance: See Cat. Nos. 69—72. The painter was responsible for most of the icons in the tier (Cat. Nos. 79—84).

Exhibitions: See Cat. Nos. 69—72.

References: See Cat. Nos. 69—72.

258

77, 78. THE APOSTLE PETER
From a Deesis tier. 15th century
115×41
Tretyakov Gallery, Moscow
Inv. No. 15057

State of preservation: Similar to the icon of *St John the Baptist* (Cat. No. 75) and most of the others in the group. A large insertion of priming with later painting in the lower part.

Iconography: Depictions of the two main Apostles St Peter and St Paul formed, together with the five central icons (including now lost icons of the Archangels which with the passage of time were replaced by the doors leading to the prothesis and diaconicon; See Cat. Nos. 85, 86), the more stable and earlier version of the Deesis tier, called the seven-figure Deesis. Not infrequently these two are the only Apostles among the other holy figures in the Deesis tier. However, in fifteenth-century Deesis tiers of larger composition, we find icons of other Apostles, mostly of St John the Divine and St Andrew (from the mid-seventh century on, after the Church reform, it was common to find a tier of just the Apostles). In this particular icon St Peter does not hold the keys to Paradise, an element to a greater extent typical of the Muscovite tradition, and which almost an invariable attribute in fifteenth-century Novgorodian painting (cf. Smirnova, Laurina, Gordiyenko 1982, ills. pp. 393, 440, 458, 470, 496). The presentation is traditional, but one of the specific features of this tier as a whole is the exaggerated number of folds in the clothing of the figures.

Provenance: See Cat. Nos. 69—72.
Exhibitions: See Cat. Nos. 69—72.
References: See Cat. Nos. 69—72.

79, 80. ST GREGORY THE DIVINE
From a Deesis tier. 15th century
116×47
Tretyakov Gallery, Moscow
Inv. No. 15060

State of preservation: Similar to the other icons in the tier. Side and upper margins partly extant. Considerable insertions of priming with later painting.

Iconography: The Church Fathers are invariably presented in expanded Deesis tiers of Russian origin or in such tiers painted in Russia by foreign artists (for instance, the late-fourteenth-century Deesis attributed to Theophanes the Greek, which is in the Cathedral of the Annunciation of the Moscow Kremlin). The most popular representations in the fifteenth century were those of St Basil the Great and St John Chrysostom. St Gregory the Divine, who was Archbishop of Constantinople (he died in 389 A.D.; see Sergius 1876, part II, pp. 29, 30), is usually partnered by St Nicholas, as is illustrated by the oldest fully extant tier of 1425—27 in the Trinity Cathedral of the Trinity-St Sergius Monastery (* V. N. Lazarev, *Andrei Rublev and His School*, Moscow, 1966, pls. 169b—171a, 176, 177; for comments on variants in the composition of the tier see also Smirnova, Laurina, Gordiyenko 1982, pp. 193—195). We may assume that the tier in question incorporated four icons with the figures of the Church Fathers. The extant depiction of St Gregory the Divine is iconographically traditional.

Provenance: See Cat. Nos. 69—72.
Exhibitions: See Cat. Nos. 69—72.
References: See Cat. Nos. 69—72.

81, 82. ST ALEXANDER OF THESSALONICA
From a Deesis tier. 15th century

116×41
Tretyakov Gallery, Moscow
Inv. No. 15061

State of preservation: Similar to other icons in the group. Side margins sawn off and considerable insertions with later painting.

Iconography: According to legend St Alexander was martyred in Thessalonica during the persecution of Christians in the early fourth century. His feast-day is November 9/22. The representation of martyrs is also customary for expanded Deesis tiers; commonest in this respect are depictions of St George and St Demetrius of Thessalonica (Cat. Nos. 83, 84). The appearance of St Alexander is most probably due to some special patronal considerations, as he was the patron saint of the fourteenth — fifteenth-century Princes Alexander Mikhailovich and Alexander Ivanovich. He figures on the seals of Tver princes (Popov 1979, pp. 141, 285). Also characteristic is his unusual dress, which is that of both warrior and martyr: thus he wears high boots, a kaftan-type tunic resembling a short dalmatic and a cloak, which has an affinity to those which Russian princes are shown wearing in icons. His pose is traditional. In the Deesis tier he was most likely partnered by another warrior saint and martyr. Hence taking into consideration the now no longer extant pairs including Archangels, Church Fathers (Cat. Nos. 79, 80) and others (Cat. Nos. 83, 84), we may assume that initially the group consisted of fifteen icons. While if it also included a second pair of Apostles, that is St Andrew and St John the Divine, as in the Trinity Cathedral iconostasis of 1425—27, then there must have been at least seventeen icons (cf. Cat. Nos. 27—33).

Provenance: See Cat. Nos. 69—72.

Exhibitions: See Cat. Nos. 69—72.

References: See Cat. Nos. 69—72.

83. ST DEMETRIUS OF THESSALONICA

From a Deesis tier. 15th century
114×42
Tretyakov Gallery, Moscow
Inv. No. 15063

State of preservation: Similar to the other icons in the group especially Cat. Nos. 79, 80.

Iconography: According to legend, the great martyr Demetrius was a soldier killed during the persecution of Christians in Thessalonica in the early fourth century (*ca.* 306 A.D., his feast-day is October 26/November 8; see Sergius 1876, part 1, pp. 340, 341). His cult is among the most popular in the Orthodox world, and in the twelfth and early thirteenth centuries, prior to the Mongol-Tartar invasion, he was especially venerated in the Vladimir-Suzdal principality. In Russian Deesis tiers he has been represented since the start of the fifteenth century (for iconography see * S. Gaidin, "The Carved Slate Icon of St Demetrius and St George", in: *Collection of Articles of the State Hermitage*, Petrograd, 1923, issue 2; A. Grabar, *L'art de la fin de l'Antiquité et du Moyen Age*, I, Paris, 1968, p. 437—460; Smirnova, Laurina, Gordiyenko 1982, pp. 221, 222, 225). The pose and dress are traditional.

Provenance: See Cat. Nos. 69—72.

Exhibitions: See Cat. Nos. 69—72.

References: See Cat. Nos. 69—72.

84. ST GEORGE

From a Deesis tier. 15th century
117×48
Tretyakov Gallery, Moscow
Inv. No. 15062

State of preservation: Similar to the other icons in the group. Side margin sawn off. Insertions with later painting in the centre and along the edges below.

Iconography: The cult of St George the Great Martyr, who was executed according to legend by the Emperor Diocletian about 303 A.D. (his feast-day is April 23/May 6), was probably the best known in the Middle Ages in both Christian and Moslem worlds. There are many apochrypha and stories about him. The image of this saint presented in literature and folklore has always attracted many experts and a considerable number of iconographic monographs have been written about him (for a summary see Lexikon 1974, vol. 6, col. 365—373; Smirnova 1976, pp. 189—191). In old Russian painting he is most commonly depicted as a warrior saint. As a rule his image is incorporated in Deesis tiers, and like St Demetrius can be found there from the early fifteenth century on.

Provenance: See Cat. Nos. 69—72.

Exhibitions: See Cat. Nos. 69—72.

References: See Cat. Nos. 69—72.

85. THE ARCHANGEL MICHAEL
Door to a prothesis (?). 15th century
111×44
Tretyakov Gallery, Moscow
Inv. No. 15058

State of preservation: Similar to the Deesis tier icons (Cat. Nos. 69—84). Lower and side margins sawn off. Major insertions with later painting on the terre-verte and central part of the figure.

Iconography: Typologically similar to the Deesis tier images (Cat. Nos. 34, 35; 36, 37). However, the panels with the figures of the Archangels Michael and Gabriel (Cat. No. 86), which have also been sawn down, were originally somewhat larger than the other icons, judging by the splines on the back. Prior to the fifteenth century nothing is known about the iconography of the side church doors, or iconostasis doors to the prothesis and diaconicon. The earliest specimen of such doors, likewise with figures of the Archangels, is from the Vladimir Cathedral of the Dormition and

is attributed to artists closely associated with Andrei Rublev and Daniil Chorny (at the Tretyakov Gallery; Antonova, Mneva 1963, 1, No. 224). On later doors of this kind, the themes depicted vary: apart from representations of the Penitent Thief, St Christopher with the head of a dog, archdeacons and Old Testament Prophet-kings, there are also other more complex themes (see Cat. No. 175). It is quite possible that such earlier doors as those of Vladimir or these from Tver were incorporated in Deesis tiers following later repair.

Provenance: See Cat. Nos. 69—72. The manner of execution — like that of Cat. No. 86 — is similar to the icons of Cat. Nos. 69—84. Despite a certain difference as regards the depiction of flesh, the door portraying the Archangel Gabriel is by the same artist, which is also confirmed by the paleographic peculiarities of the inscriptions.

Exhibitions: See Cat. Nos. 69—72.
References: See Cat. Nos. 69—72.

86. THE ARCHANGEL GABRIEL
Door to a diaconicon (?). 15th century
111×44
Tretyakov Gallery, Moscow
Inv. No. 15059

State of preservation: Similar to Cat. No. 85. A vertical crack and inset down the middle.
Iconography: See Cat. No. 85.
Provenance: See Cat. Nos. 69—72.
Exhibitions: See Cat. Nos. 69—72.
References: See Cat. Nos. 69—72.

87, 88. ST NICHOLAS WITH CHRIST AND THE VIRGIN
15th century
128×85
Rublev Museum of Early Russian Art, Moscow
Inv. No. КП 20/428

State of preservation: Heavy losses of paint due to seventeenth—nineteenth-century renovations. Upper layers greatly eroded. Major losses, with insertions of new priming below. Considerable restorative touching-up.

Iconography: The type of the central half-length figure is traditional on the whole. The roundels along the sides owe their origin to the so-called

Miracle of Nicaea, when, according to legend, Christ and the Virgin appeared to St Nicholas and presented him with the attributes of a bishop, namely an omophorion and a Gospel (see also Cat. Nos. 2—14; for a review of similar iconographic approaches in Russian and Balkan painting of the preceding period see Smirnova 1976, pp. 151—153).

Provenance: Presumably from the Tver Church of the Presentation in the Temple. When it entered the Tver Museum is unknown; in 1964 it was transferred from what was by then the Kalinin Museum of Local Lore to the Rublev Museum (the original name of Tver has now been restored to the city).

Exhibitions: 1969—70 Moscow
References: Vzdornov 1970, p. 358, ill.
p. 359; Tver Painting 1970, p. 20
(No. 10); Popov 1970, pp. 339, 340,
ill. p. 341; Yevseyeva, Kochetkov,
Sergeyev 1974, pp. 26, 27 (*Ibid.* 1983,
pp. 21, 22); Popov 1979, pp. 145, 184,
289, 290, ills. pp. 146, 147, 402,
403; Saltykov 1981, pp. 15, 243, ill. 20

89, 90. THE ENTRY INTO JERUSALEM
15th century
61×44
Cathedral of the Intercession of the
Virgin in the Rogozhskoye Cemetery,
Moscow

State of preservation: Good on the
whole. Insertions of new priming in
the margins, minor losses, insertions
and painting abraded over the entire
surface.

Iconography: Traditional for fifteenth-
century Russian painting (see Cat.
Nos. 53—55). Specific features include
the many figures of children tearing
off palm branches and welcoming
Christ at the gates. In the centre
in the foreground is the scene of "the
extraction of the splinter" (encountered in twelfth- and thirteenth-century Balkan monumental painting, but
especially common in the Paleologue
epoch: Dufrenne 1972, p. 24; for
variants of the playing children see
E. L. Palli, "Einzug in Jerusalem", in:
Reallexikon 1967, vol. 2, issue 9,
col. 28). In fifteenth-century Russian
painting a similar version is to be
found in a tablet painted in Novgorod
late in the century (* V. N. Lazarev,
*Pages from the History of Novgorod-
ian Painting. Bilateral Tablets from
the Novgorod Cathedral of St Sophia*,
Moscow, 1977, pl. XIII). The stone
face embellishing the Jerusalem
wall in this icon also derives from
a Balkan source (Popov 1979,
pp. 131—133, 288).

Provenance: Entered the Cathedral of
the Intercession of the Virgin in
1917 from the collection of the
Rakhmanovs, a family of Old Believers.
Despite the undoubted resemblance
to fifteenth-century Tver painting,
the attribution proposed is still
slightly hypothetical. Because of the
icon's size it is possible that it may
have been commissioned as a patronal
icon for a small church. However,
suggestions that it comes from a
Church Feasts tier appear closer to
the truth.

References: * D. A. Rovinsky, *Review
of Icon-Painting up to the Close of
the Seventeenth Century. Description
of Fireworks Displays and Carnival
Lights*, St Petersburg, 1903, p. 18,
note 1; * *Old Icons of the Old-Believer
Cathedral of the Intercession of the
Virgin at the Rogozhskoye Cemetery
in Moscow*, Moscow, 1956, p. 13, pl. 5;
Antonova, Mneva 1963, 1, p. 316,
note 1; Popov 1970, p. 342, note 86;
Popov 1979, pp. 110, 131—133, 287,
288, ills. pp. 398—401; Smirnova,
Laurina, Gordiyenko 1982, p. 313

91—94. THE SYNAXIS (LAUDATION) OF THE VIRGIN
Second half of the 15th century. Tver (?)
85×66
P. D. Korin Memorial Museum, a
branch of the Tretyakov Gallery,
Moscow
Inv. No. ДР 373

State of preservation: As the result
of several renovations and
unsuccessful restorations the glazing,
highlights and golden ground are
largely eroded. Losses of priming,
insertions, heavy crackling. Numerous
minor touchings-up, even overpainting
below and where there are insets of
priming down the middle of the icon.

Iconography: The theme is an illustration of a long Christmas canticle
(see Cat. Nos. 38—43) ascribed to the
Byzantine theologian, philosopher and
poet St John Damascene (*ca.* 650—
before 754). The Synaxis of the Virgin
is celebrated the day after Christmas.
In the centre there is a sphere
enclosing the enthroned Virgin and
Infant Christ; in front is a group of
singers, on the left-hand side, St John
Damascene and on the right-hand side,
Cosmas of Mayum; next to them are
scenes in which the Earth 'offers'
Christ the cave and the Wilderness
with the manger, while in the upper
left- and right-hand corners we see
respectively the Three Wise Men
(the Magi) bearing gifts, and the
shepherds; while the entire scene is
crowned by the celestial sphere with
depictions of angels and the Holy Ghost
descending. This complex composition

evolved in thirteenth-century painting and is regarded as a manifestation of the new Paleologue artistic outlook (Pokrovsky 1892, pp. 88, 89; G. Millet, *Recherches sur l'iconographie de l'Evangile*, Paris, 1916, pp. 163—169; L. Mirković, *Kheortologiya ili istoriyski razvitak i bogosluzhenie prazdnika pravoslavne i stoyane tsrkve*, Belgrade, 1961, p. 93, in Serbian; V. Djurić, *Vizantiyske freske u Yugoslaviyu*, Belgrade, 1975, p. 202, note 50, in Serbian). This icon represents one of the very first reproductions of the Laudation scene in Russian painting; there is, true, a Pskovian icon, of still earlier date but it too was painted not before the beginning of the fifteenth century (Antonova, Mneva 1963, 1, pls. 101, 102); however, in the icon here the treatment is different and closer to Balkan variants. Subsequently, this theme along with other hymnographical compositions of the Mariological cycle became common and widespread. One closely associated iconographic variant is presented in the wall-paintings of the St Therapont Monastery Cathedral of the Nativity, created by the Muscovite artist Dionysius in 1502—03. Judging by what remains of the inscription, the painter himself termed the icon from the Korin collection the "Laudation of the Mother of God"; that though is wrong, as the Laudation deals with the extolling of the Virgin and the Infant Jesus by the Prophets and possesses a definite transfigurative aspect (cf. the wall-paintings of the 1480s in the Cathedral of the Dormition of the Moscow Kremlin and a presumably late-fourteenth-century Serbian icon; see * *An Exhibition Catalogue of Byzantine Art in USSR Collections*, Moscow, 1977, vol. 3, No. 972; * T. V. Tolstaya, *The Moscow Kremlin Cathedral of the Dormition*, Moscow, 1977, ills. 58, 59, 80).

Provenance: Before being acquired by Korin the icon belonged to the well-known architect A. V. Shchusev. The attribution proposed is based on researches by Tretyakov Gallery staff members V. V. Nartsissov and L. I. Lifshits; but it is undeniably hypothetical, since such complex Mariological composition was not popular in fifteenth-century Tver, except for the time of Vassian Strigin-Obolensky, who was closely associated with Muscovite circles in the Church and was, in 1461—77, Archimandrite of the Otroch Monastery and subsequently Bishop of Tver (for the illuminated Gospel Book of 1478 that he commissioned see the introduction, ills. 29, 30). The present icon may be dated to approximately the same period, i.e. the third quarter of the fifteenth century.

Exhibitions: 1969 Moscow
References: Onasch 1961, pl. 33, note p. 361; * V. I. Antonova, *Early Russian Art in the Korin Collection*, Moscow, 1967, pp. 38, 39, ill. 30; Rostov-Suzdalian Painting 1967, p. 12, ill. p. 26; * *The Tretyakov Gallery. Exhibition of Pre-Revolutionary Russian and Soviet Art (Painting, Sculpture, Graphic Works). New Acquisitions. 1963—1968. Catalogue*, Moscow, 1969, p. 22; * V. I. Djurić, "Portraits in the Representations of Christmas Hymns", in: *Byzantium. The Southern Slavs and Ancient Rus. Western Europe*, Moscow, 1973, p. 254, note 10; Popov 1975, p. 59, pl. 73; * M. A. Orlova, "The *Nativity* from the Korin Collection", *Early Russian Art. 14th—15th Centuries*, Moscow, 1984, pp. 258, 259, 263, ill. p. 259

95, 96. THE VIRGIN

From a Deesis tier. Second half of the 15th century

108×41

Tretyakov Gallery, Moscow
Inv. No. 21458

State of preservation: Good on the whole with minor insertions and touching up.

Iconography: Traditional for full-length Deesis icons, with a manner of drawing similar to Muscovite pieces of the fifteenth and early sixteenth centuries (see Cat. Nos. 27—33; 73, 74).

Provenance: Like its companion icon of *St John the Baptist* (Cat. Nos. 97—100), it is from the Old-Believer chapel in Uglich, from which it entered the local Museum of Regional Studies, then, in 1934, was transferred to the Tretyakov Gallery. The earlier, presumably Tver, icon of *St Barbara* (Cat. Nos. 10, 11) is of the same provenance. Although neither of the two Deesis tier icons can now be considered pure Tver workmanship, since they are virtually in the mainstream of the general Russian trend, almost Muscovite in style, they still stand in a clear line of continuity from the icons of Tver's Cathedral of the Transfiguration (Cat. Nos. 27—68). Both are by the same painter.

Exhibitions: 1960 Moscow; 1973—74 Moscow; 1976 Leningrad

References: * A. Svirin, *Early Russian Painting in the Collection of the State Tretyakov Gallery*, Moscow, 1958, ills. 50, 51; Rublev Exhibition 1960, pp. 14, 44 (No. 91), ill. 23; Antonova, Mneva 1963, 1, pp. 325, 326 (No. 270), pl. 213; Popov 1977, pp. 260, 262, ill. p. 257; Popov 1979, pp. 174, 177, 305—307, ills. pp. 173, 306; Dionysius 1981, p. 31 (No. 14)

97—100. ST JOHN THE BAPTIST
From a Deesis tier. Second half of the 15th century

108×41

Tretyakov Gallery, Moscow
Inv. No. 21446

State of preservation: Similar to Cat. Nos. 95, 96.

Iconography: The ascetic variant traditional for fifteenth-century painting (see Cat. No. 75). In its details the drawing bears a close resemblance to Deesis icons painted by artists of the Rublev circle for Vladimir and the Trinity-St Sergius Monastery and also to the iconostasis painted by Dionysius in 1502—03 for the St Therapont Monastery, although structurally it is more precise. The text on the scroll is from the Gospels (Matthew III, 2; IV, 17; Luke III, 9).

Provenance: See Cat. Nos. 95, 96.

Exhibitions: See Cat. Nos. 95, 96.

References: See Cat. Nos. 95, 96.

101—103. THE OLD TESTAMENT TRINITY. 1484—85. Tver—Moscow
By master Paisii

152.5×119.5

Rublev Museum of Early Russian Art, Moscow
Inv. No. Вр. п. 21

State of preservation: Many eroded sections of painting, in places down to the preparatory sketch, the results of crude restoration work in the 1880s. Minor losses of priming. Many traces of nails from the mounting. During the most recent restoration, the losses in the field and landscape were touched up to approximate the original painting, which is less in evidence on the figures and the building.

Iconography: The theme derives from an Old Testament text (Genesis XVIII) and is among the earliest in Christian art (mentioned in the early fourth century, with the oldest extant example dating from the late fourth century. There is an Orthodox feast of the Trinity eight weeks after Easter (cf. Cat. Nos. 61, 62). When the Second Ecumenical Council affirmed the dogma of the Holy Trinity in 381, this theme and concept became basic to the religious view of the world. Hence the frequency with which it occurs and the heated disputes over its symbolical meaning and the interpretation of the God the Father, God the Holy Ghost and God the Son. The representation of the Trinity, otherwise known as the Hospitality of Abraham (see Cat. Nos. 119, 120), goes back as far as the eleventh-century wall-paintings in the Kiev Cathedral of St Sophia, and persisted until the seventeenth century. It acquired particular popularity after Andrei Rublev most probably produced his celebrated icon around 1411, with all subsequent artists taking his work as a point of reference to some extent or another. Paisii's work is a direct copy of Rublev's icon, with the exception of some artistic and dogmatic alterations, for instance, the three chalices (for other copies see Popov 1979, pp. 310, 311; and the bibliography of iconographic studies of the Rublev icon in an anthology compiled by G. I. Vzdornov, Moscow, 1981, pp. 133—135, ills. 1—52). Apart from the pictorial illustration of the Old Testament text, there is also a New Testament version on the theme of the Trinity known as the Paternity (Smirnova 1976, pp. 234, 235).

Provenance: From the Cathedral of the

Dormition of the Monastery of St Joseph of Volokolamsk, near the town of the same name, where it had been in the Local tier of the iconostasis. It entered the Rublev Museum in 1954, and has been dated to the period when the Cathedral was painted. The 1545 Monastery inventory names the painter as Paisii, who was evidently a local monk. The style is directly linked to that of the icons from Tver's Cathedral of the Transfiguration (Cat. Nos. 27—68), but, like the Deesis tier icons of the third quarter of the fifteenth century (Cat. Nos. 95, 96; 97—100), it bears a resemblance to contemporary Muscovite painting and is a product of the new conditions in which the artist was working. Though Paisii may have been a member of the Kashin team, or perhaps an apprentice there, he is also already a fully Muscovite artist.

Exhibitions: 1976 Leningrad

References: * Nectarius, Hieromonk, *A Historical Description of the Second-Class Monastery of St Joseph of Volokolamsk in the Moscow Gubernia*, Moscow, 1887, p. 31; * V. T. Georgievsky, *Frescoes of the St Therapont Monastery*, St Petersburg, 1911, fig. 15, appendix, p. 1 (1545 Monastery inventory); Popov 1971, pp. 106, 107; Popov 1973, p. 84; Popov 1975, pp. 74, 93, pls. 129, 130; Popov 1977, p. 262, ill. p. 261; Sergeyev 1977, pp. 259—261; Popov 1979, pp. 177, 200, 205—212, 308—311, ills. pp. 207, 209, 434, 435; Dionysius 1981, p. 33 (No. 19); Saltykov 1981, pp. 25, 245, ills. 49, 50; * *Andrei Rublev's "Trinity". An Anthology*, compiled by G. I. Vzdornov, Moscow, 1981, p. 141, ill. 43 * V. A. Meniaylo, "The Icons by the Monk Paisii in the Monastery of St Joseph of Volokolamsk", in: *Materials of Scientific Conferences: 1989—90*, Moscow, 1991, issue 1

104. ROYAL DOORS. SCENE: THE EVANGELIST MATTHEW AND SANCTA SOPHIA THE HOLY WISDOM
Second half of the 15th century
52×37.5
Russian Museum, St Petersburg
Inv. No. држ. 1408

State of preservation: Good. Loss of painting and priming in margins and field. Minor touching up.

Iconography: The 'mirror' image of the depiction in Cat. No. 105, with only the type of buildings altered; the vellum between them, which is absent in Cat. No. 105, is a characteristic detail in illuminations depicting the Evangelists but is more seldom encountered in Royal Doors scenes. The altered position of the book held by the Holy Wisdom (cf. Cat. No. 105) indicates that the writing of the Gospel was conceived as copying from the book thus held, whereas in Cat. No. 105 the process is construed as the recording of dictation. The text is from Matthew I, 1.

Provenance: From the collection of V. A. Prokhorov from which it entered the museum in 1898.

Exhibitions: 1967—68 Paris; 1973 Budapest; 1974 Helsinki

References: * *Inventory of Russian Antiquities Comprising V. A. Prokhorov's Collection*, St Petersburg, 1896, p. 34 (No. 701); * *Review of Christian Antiquities in the Emperor Alexander III Museum*, St Petersburg, 1902, p. 36 (N. P. Likhachev wrote the section *A Brief Description of the Icons in Rooms XIX—XXI*); L'art russe des Scythes à nos jours 1967, No. 248; Popov 1970, p. 326, note 41; *Regi orosz müvéezet kiàllitàs, Budapest, Szépmüvészeti Múseum, 1973*, Budapest, 1973, pp. 6, 10 (No. 2), ill. 1; *Venäjän taidetta 900—1600—luvuilta Valtion Eremitaasin ja Valtion Venäläisen museon kokoelmista*, Helsinki, 1974, No. 114; Popov 1979, pp. 128, 131ff, 184—186, 192, 315—317, ills. pp. 180, 438; Smirnova 1983, p. 188

105. ROYAL DOORS. LEFT LEAF SCENES: THE ANNUNCIATION; THE EVANGELIST JOHN AND ST PROCHORUS; THE EVANGELIST LUKE AND SANCTA SOPHIA THE HOLY WISDOM
Second half of the 15th century
138×31.5
Rublev Museum of Early Russian Art, Moscow
Inv. No. КП 17/43

State of preservation: Patchy and uneven. Considerable losses of priming in the upper marginal scene (part of the Annunciation) and in the margins. Losses of priming in the marginal scenes, abrasions of the paint layer, heavy crackling.

Iconography: Both scenes illustrate the writing of the Gospel text. The representation of the Evangelists was together with the Church Fathers as

creators of the Liturgy (see Cat. Nos. 25, 26) one of the most popular ways of decorating the Royal Doors. Throughout the fifteenth century, the type seen here with four scenes on the two leaves persists, but towards the close of the century and later, one more tier was not infrequently added representing the Eucharist, the Communion of the Apostles. The closest analogies are to be found in contemporary book illumination and some icons from the turn of the sixteenth century. One scene depicts the Evangelist John with St Prochorus against the background on the Island of Patmos, where according to legend St John wrote the Gospel associated with his name and the Book of the Revelation; the rays from the Holy Ghost emphasize divine inspiration. In the second scene, though, divine inspiration is personified by the Holy Wisdom or Sancta Sophia as a wingless angel; though iconographically rarer, this too is not absolutely unique in the second half of the fifteenth century (a large body of literature is devoted to the personification of the Holy Wisdom that derives from the muses of Antiquity; Popov 1979, pp. 314, 315;

Smirnova 1963, pp. 180—189). The text in the second scene is from Luke I, 1.

Provenance: Presumably from the Church of the Nativity of the Virgin in Tver's Yamskaya Quarter (see also Cat. Nos. 69—72). In 1897 the leaf entered the Tver Museum and in 1964 was transferred by what was then the Kalinin Museum of Local Lore to the Rublev Museum.

Exhibitions: 1969—70 Moscow

References: Ivanova, Kukles, Popov 1968, p. 32, ill. p. 33; Vzdornov 1970, p. 358; Tver Painting 1970, p. 26 (No. 21); Popov 1969/70, p. 322, note 18; Popov 1970, pp. 317, 324, 326, 327, ill. p. 318, pl. between p. 316 and p. 317; Yevseyeva, Kochetkov, Sergeyev 1974, pp. 37, 38, pls. 51, 52 (*Ibid.* 1983, pp. 33, 34, pls. 65, 66); Popov 1979, pp. 138, 172, 177—180, 183—186, 312—315, ills. pp. 181, 436, 437; Saltykov 1981, pp. 16, 243, ills. 18, 19; Lazarev 1983, p. 130; Smirnova 1983, p. 188

106—112. THE DORMITION
Last quarter of the 15th century
113×88
Tretyakov Gallery, Moscow
Inv. No. 22303

State of preservation: Good. Minor losses and abrasions of the paint layer. Touching up during restoration.

Iconography: Representative of the 'cloud' type of Dormition that was popular in Russian icon-painting of the second half of the fifteenth century, but had a long history in Byzantine-Balkan painting. The basic elements of the composition, including the group of Apostles and angels riding on clouds, and the scene in which Thomas receives the girdle from the ascending Virgin, derive from apocrypha and are more specifically associated with the texts of a sermon ascribed to St John the Divine, the canons of Cosmas of Mayum (seventh—eighth centuries) and St John Damascene as well as of the mid-fourteenth-century Acathistos to the Dormition (for theme and iconography see Porfiryev 1890, pp. 76—96, 270—279; Dufrenne 1972, pp. 26—28; Lexikon 1972, vol. 4; Smirnova 1976, pp. 228—230). The present icon differs from contemporary,

chiefly Muscovite, works in taking its orientation from early iconographic variants and its omission of a number of episodes, such as the punishment of Aphonius, and figures, with two bishops instead of four, no angels, etc. (for more detail see Popov 1979, p. 230).

Provenance: Entered the Tretyakov Gallery from the Ostroukhov Museum of Icon-Painting and Painting in 1929 (acquired by the collector in Minsk before the Revolution). Several stories are related as to how the icon came to Minsk, the most likely suggesting a link with Tver's last Prince, Mikhail Borisovich, who stayed there on his flight to Lithuania in 1485. An analysis of the style warrants our ascribing it with certainty to a Tver artist (see the introductory article for mention of the Tver Prince's court in Lithuania and Poland).

Exhibitions: 1958 Moscow; 1960 Moscow; 1969—70 Moscow; 1976 Leningrad

References: Nekrasov 1937, p. 186, fig. 125; * *The Tretyakov Gallery: Catalogue of Art Works on Display*, Moscow, 1947, p. 28; Voronin, Lazarev 1955, pp. 31—33, ill. p. 33; USSR. Russian Icons 1958, pp. 10,

25, 26, pl. XVI; Yagodovskaya 1958, p. 49; Rublev Exhibition 1960, pp. 16, 41 (No. 75); Onasch 1961, pl. 116, note p. 394; Antonova, Mneva 1963, I, No. 201, pp. 235, 236, pls. 140, 141; L'art russe des Scythes à nos jours 1967, No. 249; Vzdornov 1970, p. 358; Tver Painting 1970, p. 21, No. 12; Popov 1970, pp. 340, 342, ill. p. 343; Popov 1973, p. 85; Yevseyeva, Kochetkov, Sergeyev 1974, pp. 28, 29, pls. 26—29; Idem 1983, pp. 29, 30, pls. 53—56; Popov 1979, pp. 131, 172, 189, 319—321, ills. 191, 440, 441; * N. F. Vysotskaya, T. A. Karpovich, *Painting of Byelorussia. 12th—18th Centuries*, Minsk, 1980, pls. 14—16; Dionysius 1981, p. 30 (No. 10); Yevseyeva 1981, pp. 65, 66; Popov 1982, pp. 309, 310; Lazarev 1983, p. 131

113. ST JOHN THE DIVINE
Second half of the 15th century. Tver (?)

48×34

Russian Museum, St Petersburg
Inv. No. држ. 1601

State of preservation: Uneven. Losses of priming above and below and also along the lower edge of the half-length figure. Numerous traces of nails from the mounting. Paint layer considerably eroded and abraded in places. Additions to priming and touchings-up. Drawing partly corrected — a so-called collector's restoration.

Iconography: Frontal half-length portrayals of the Apostle in the act of blessing are rare in early Russian painting (see Popov 1979, p. 318). The icon of St John, whose feast-day is 8/21 May, was most likely the patronal icon of a small church.

Provenance: From the collection of N. P. Likhachev. Entered the museum in 1913.

References: * N. P. Likhachev, *Andrei Rublev's Manner*, St Petersburg, 1907, p. 55 (No. 27); Popov 1979, pp. 186—189, 193, 222, 317, 318, ill. p. 439

114—116. CHRIST PANTOCRATOR
From a half-length Deesis tier. Last quarter of the 15th century

84×60

Tver Picture Gallery
Inv. No. Ж-1007

State of preservation: Good with minor losses in the margins and on the dress, traces of nails around head and halo from the crescent crown, and touching up during restoration.

Iconography: Belongs to the half-length Deesis type that was widely current in fourteenth- and fifteenth-century Byzantine and Russian art (see Cat. Nos. 6, 7). Specific details in the handling of forms, including the Gospel held in the left hand, indicate an imitation of the Balkan prototype.

Provenance: From the Church of the Lama Cemetery outside Vesiegonsk, where it was found among other icons brought later. In 1935 it entered the Vesiegonsk Museum and in 1938, the Kalinin Picture Gallery. No information is available with regard to the other icons (Cat. Nos. 117, 118) from the same tier.

Exhibitions: 1969—70 Moscow; 1972 Moscow

References: * V. I. Antonova, "At Lake Medvezhya and Vesiegonsk", *Transactions of the Department of Early Russian Literature*. Vol. 22. *The Interaction of Literature and the Visual Arts in Old Russia*, Moscow — Leningrad, 1966, pp. 195—198, 202, fig. 1; Ivanova, Kukles, Popov 1968, p. 36, ill. p. 37; Ivanova 1969, pls. 14, 15; Tver Painting 1970, p. 27 (No. 22); Popov 1970, pp. 344—346, ill. p. 347; Briusova 1974, p. 186, note 30; Yevseyeva, Kochetkov, Sergeyev 1974, pp. 21, 22, pls. 16—21; Idem 1983, pp. 18, 19; * G. V. Popov, "Periodization of 15th-Century Russo-Balkans Ties (Based on Painting and Illumination)", *Slav Cultures and the Balkans*, Sofia, 1, 1978, No. 283, fig. 4; Gusarova 1979, pp. 112—114, 119, 125; Popov 1979, pp. 156, 172, 189, 194—200, 321—325, ills. pp. 195, 197, 442, 443; Yevseyeva 1981, pp. 56—68; * V. N. Sergeyev, "Concerning the Attribution of the Fifteenth-Century Icon of the Apostle Paul from the Village of Chamerovo", in: *Early Russian Art of the 15th—17th Centuries*, Moscow, 1981, pp. 155, 156; Saltykov 1981, p. 243, ill. 23; Popov 1982, pp. 309, 310, 312; Smirnova, Laurina, Gordiyenko 1982, pp. 30, 77

117, 118. THE APOSTLE PAUL
From a half-length Deesis tier. Last quarter of the 15th century

84×59

Rublev Museum of Early Russian Art, Moscow

Inv. No. КП 994/333

State of preservation: Though similar to Cat. Nos. 114—116, on the whole the surface is covered with later scratched lines duplicating the contours — probably traces of eighteenth-century repair — which coarsened the original draughtsmanship.

Iconography: Traditional for half-length Deesis representations in Balkan-orientated Russian painting of the fifteenth century (Popov 1979, pp. 322, 324, 325; Yevseyeva 1981, p. 58).

Provenance: From the village of Chernetskoye, from which it was transferred to the village church of Chamerovo near Vesiegonsk in the neighbourhood of Tver. Acquired by the Rublev Museum in 1963.

Exhibitions: 1967 Archaeology; 1969—70 Moscow; 1972 Moscow

References: See Cat. Nos. 114—116.

119, 120. THE OLD TESTAMENT TRINITY (fragments).
***Ca.* early 16th century**

67.5×56

Tretyakov Gallery, Moscow

Inv. No. 15253

State of preservation: Patchy. Considerable insertions of later priming with painting done in 1826, as is indicated by an inscription along the lower edge.

Iconography: Here the theme of the Hospitality of Abraham is strictly presented — in contrast to symbolical versions but in accordance with the biblical text. Abraham and Sarah are shown serving the angels and the killing of the calf is depicted in the foreground. Variations of this iconographic type were popular in Russian art in the thirteenth and fourteenth centuries and experienced a revival in the sixteenth century as the philosophical impact of the Rublev tradition faded (see Cat. Nos. 101—103 and also Popov 1979, pp. 350, 351).

Provenance: From the Tver Church of the White Trinity. Entered the Tver Museum before 1926, was transferred to the Moscow Central Restoration Workshops in 1927, and in 1934 was passed to the Tretyakov Gallery. As the Church of the White Trinity was built in the 1560s, the icon was usually dated to that period, and this was supported by the inscription added in 1826, when the icon was refurbished, supposedly in reproduction of an original, which gave the date of painting as 1561 and claimed that the icon was commissioned by a certain Nechai. Evidently this came about as a result of a misunderstanding, since the style would suggest a date in the early sixteenth century. Also in the Tretyakov Gallery is another icon on the same theme from the same church, carrying a similar later apocryphal inscription ascribing it to the hand of "Andrei Rublev the former royal Muscovite master"; possibly the date indicated in the inscription on the present icon should in fact apply to the second (cf. Popov 1979, pp. 351—354). While the second icon, which is from the mid-sixteenth century, may be by a Muscovite painter, this icon is undoubtedly in the mainstream of Tver tradition.

Exhibitions: 1969—70 Moscow

References: Vladislavlev 1863, p. 114; * *The Journal of the 66th Session of the Academic Archives Commission of Tver*, Tver, 1896, p. 7; Nekrasov 1900, p. 13; Pogozheva 1914, p. 43; Rublev Exhibition 1960, p. 11, note 3; Antonova, Mneva 1963, 1, No. 244 (pp. 303, 304); Tver Painting 1970, p. 35 (No. 39); Popov 1970, p. 336; Yevseyeva, Kochetkov, Sergeyev 1974, pl. 73; Idem 1983, p. 36; Popov 1979, pp. 143, 215, 232, 248—351, ill. p. 463

121. THE VIRGIN HODEGETRIA
Relief-carved icon. First third of the 16th century

27.5×25.5 and 42×35.5 with base

Rublev Museum of Early Russian Art, Moscow

Inv. No. 292/953

State of preservation: Good on the whole with minor additions and restorative touching up, chiefly of the gilding.

Iconography: Traditional for the fifteenth and sixteenth centuries (see Cat. Nos. 12—14; 24).

Provenance: In the 1920s the icon was in the Monastery of St Nicholas of the Kamelaukion near Kashin, which is first mentioned in documents from the turn of the sixteenth century (see *P. Stroyev, *Register of Hierarchs and Abbots of Monasteries of the Russian Church*, St Petersburg, 1877, col. 466). Entered the Rublev Museum in 1962 from the Mosfilm Studios.

Exhibitions: 1964 Moscow; 1969—70 Moscow

References: *Exhibition of Russian Wooden Sculpture and Carvings. Catalogue*, Moscow, 1964, pp. 24, 25; N. N. Pomerantsev, *Russian Wooden Sculpture* (in Russian & English), Moscow, 1967, pl. 8; Tver Painting 1970, p. 26 (No. 20); Yevseyeva, Kochetkov, Sergeyev 1974, pp. 31, 32, pl. 43 (*Ibid*. 1983, pp. 24, 25, pl. 39); Ryndina 1979, pp. 481, 536, 586, 587, ills. pp. 535, 614

122. THE VIRGIN HODEGETRIA
First third of the 16th century

35.5×28.5
Museum of History and Art, Sergiyev Posad
Inv. No. 4961

State of preservation: Good with minor abrasions of the paint layer and partial loss of the sixteenth-century silver repoussé embellishment on the lower ground.

Iconography: A classic variant for the fifteenth and sixteenth centuries, similar to the earlier Tver icon that bears a mention of the name of Anna Mikulinskaya (Cat. No. 24).

Provenance: From the sacristy of the Trinity-St Sergius Monastery.

References: Olsufyev 1920, p. 78 (No. N/233); Nikolayeva 1977, p. 79 (No. 105), ill.; Popov 1979, p. 248

123, 124. CHRIST IN MAJESTY
From a Deesis tier. First third of the 16th century

123×91
Tver Picture Gallery
Inv. No. Ж-1115

State of preservation: Cracks and losses of priming along the panel joints; the right hand to wrist, a portion of the sleeve and the gilding of the halo almost completely lost. Considerable restorative touching up.

Iconography: Traditional for central full-length Deesis tier icons (see Cat. No. 27—33). The text displayed (see Cat. Nos. 27—33; 69—72) is from John VII, 24; Matthew VII, 1—2.

Provenance: The central icon of the Deesis tier (see Cat. Nos. 125, 126; 127, 128) from the Old-Believer Church of the Dormition in Tver, which entered the Gallery together with the other icons in 1941. According to archaeological finds, another church stood on this site in the early sixteenth century. The tier also included an icon of *St Gregory the Divine*,

which may, however, date from the turn of the sixteenth century, and a much later icon of *St Basil the Great* which is also now in the Gallery (Popov 1979, pp. 249, 333, 342, ill. p. 459).

Exhibitions: 1969—70 Moscow

References: Tver Painting 1970, p. 33 (No. 33); Popov 1970, p. 352, note 108; Yevseyeva, Kochetkov, Sergeyev 1974, p. 41, pl. 71, 72 (*Ibid*. 1983, p. 36); Popov 1979, pp. 141, 221, 227—229, 333—335, ills. pp. 452—455

125, 126. THE VIRGIN
From a Deesis tier. First third of the 16th century

123×56
Tver Picture Gallery
Inv. No. Ж-1119

State of preservation: Similar to Cat. Nos. 123, 124 with considerable restorative touching up.
Iconography: Traditional for the fifteenth and sixteenth centuries (see Cat. Nos. 27—33; 73, 74).
Provenance: See Cat. Nos. 123, 124.
Exhibitions: See Cat. Nos. 123, 124.
References: See Cat. Nos. 123, 124.

127, 128. ST JOHN THE ALMSGIVER
From a Deesis tier. First third of the 15th century

123×53
Tver Picture Gallery
Inv. No. Ж-1121

State of preservation: Similar to Cat. Nos. 125, 126 with considerable restorative additions and touching up.
Iconography: St John the Almsgiver, who died in 616—620, was Patriarch of Alexandria in the early seventh century. His feast-day is 12/25 November (see Sergius 1876, part 2, p. 357). No other icons of him are known in fifteenth- and sixteenth-century Deesis tiers. His image was more common in Novgorodian painting (Smirnova, Laurina, Gordiyenko 1982, p. 272). Its appearance in the Tver Deesis tier, like that of the earlier icon of *St Alexander of Thessalonica* (Cat. Nos. 81, 82) may have been due the wishes of a particular patron or a local cult that possibly sprang up in the early fifteenth century. According to a census taken in 1616, a church consecrated to St John the Almsgiver stood in the heart of the city.
Provenance: See Cat. Nos. 123, 124.
Exhibitions: See Cat. Nos. 123, 124.
References: See Cat. Nos. 123, 124.

129—133. ST PARASCEVE PIATNITSA WITH SCENES FROM HER LIFE
First half of the 16th century

74×54
Rublev Museum of Early Russian Art, Moscow
Inv. No. 252/435

State of preservation: The marginal scenes are in a better state than the centre which has major losses and numerous insertions of new priming and touching up, with the exception of the bottom row which also shows considerable restorative additions.
Iconography: Parasceve Piatnitsa from Iconium in Asia Minor is said to have been martyred in the time of Diocletian (284—305). Her feast-day is October 28/November 10. One characteristic feature is the wreath that she wears (Onasch 1961, pp. 352, 353, also Smirnova, Laurina, Gordiyenko 1982, pp. 237—239). She is often confused with another Roman martyr of the same name, whose feast-day is July 26/August 8. Her cult was commonest in the lands of Novgorod and Pskov; the earliest hagiographical icons of Russian origin date from the same period as this icon. The marginal scenes have a rather complicated arrangement with the fourth in the upper row being followed by the one immediately below on the right-hand side, which is in turn followed by the one opposite on the left, while the seventh is directly left below. The eighth scene is again opposite on the right below which comes the ninth and then the tenth back on the left-hand side; following which come the last five marginal scenes in the bottom row. They depict: 1) The birth of St Parasceve; 2) Her giving away her wealth after the death of her parents and preaching Christianity to the populace; 3) Incarceration in a dungeon; 4) St Parasceve is brought before the king; 5) She is flogged with bull whips; 6) The Virgin appears in shining glory with angels to St Parasceve in the dungeon; 7) The king converses with

St Parasceve; 8) She continues to talk with the king; 9) She is strung up on a tree; 10) She destroys a pagan shrine and its idols; 11) She is again brought before the king; 12) She is tortured with flames ('candles'); 13) She is beheaded; 14) The king perishes for having broken the law; 15) The burial of St Parasceve.

Provenance: From the church in the village of Porechye near Bezhetsk in Tver Region from which it entered the Rublev Museum in 1965.

Exhibitions: 1969—70 Moscow

References: Ivanova, Kukles, Popov 1968, ills. pp. 25, 27; Ivanova 1969, p. 14, pls. 9—13; * I. A. Kochetkov, "The Word and the Image in a Hagiographical Icon", *Transactions of the Department of Old Russian Literature*, Leningrad, 1969, vol. 34, pp. 159—162; Tver Painting 1970, pp. 31, 32 (No. 30); Popov 1970, pp. 317, 318, 351, 352, ill. p. 323; * L. M. Yevseyeva, V. N. Sergeyev, *Guide to the Andrei Rublev Museum of Early Russian Art*, Moscow, 1971, pp. 43, 44, ill. p. 45; Yevseyeva, Kochetkov, Sergeyev 1974, pp. 39—41, pls. 54, 55 (*Ibid.* 1983, pp. 34, 35, pl. 68); Popov 1979, pp. 221, 228, 229, 336—340, ills. pp. 456, 457; Saltykov 1981, pp. 35, 247, 248, ills. 95, 96; Smirnova, Laurina, Gordiyenko 1982, pp. 238, 239

134, 135. THE ARCHANGEL GABRIEL
From a Deesis tier. First half of the 16th century

131×59
Rublev Museum of Early Russian Art, Moscow
Inv. No. 18/430

State of preservation: Losses of painting, especially glazing in places, with the background, terre-verte and margins worst eroded. Insertions of new priming painted over during restoration.

Iconography: Traditional on the whole for Deesis icons (see Cat. Nos. 34, 35; 36, 37; 85, 86). The variant with clavus, deriving from the Byzantine tradition of court ceremony, is less common, although Archangels dressed in this way are known in Russian painting from the eleventh century. However, it is the type wearing the chiton and himation that prevails in Russian Deesis icons (for more detail see Popov 1979, pp. 341, 342).

Provenance: From an unknown Tver church. Entered the local museum in 1903 and the Rublev Museum in 1964.

Exhibitions: 1969—70 Moscow

References: Tver Painting 1970, pp. 30, 31 (No. 28); Popov 1970, p. 348; Yevseyeva, Kochetkov, Sergeyev 1974, p. 41, pl. 70; Idem 1983, p. 36, pl. 69; Popov 1979, pp. 221, 229, 327, 340—342, ill. p. 458; Saltykov 1981, pp. 40, 248, ill. 100

136. ST SABBATHEUS OF TVER (OF ORSHA)
Ca. mid-16th century

25.5×21
Rublev Museum of Early Russian Art, Moscow
Inv. No. КП 1535

State of preservation: Good with minor losses of paint layer and priming, traces of nails from mounting, filled in and touched up to reproduce the original painting.

Iconography: St Sabbatheus of Tver, who lived at the close of the fourteenth century and in the first half of the fifteenth and who is, unreliably, reported to have died in 1434, took his vows at the Orsha Monastery near Tver. According to legend he made a pilgrimage to Jerusalem, from which he returned with a wooden cross. We do not know exactly when he founded the Monastery of the Presentation in the Temple on the banks of the same Orsha River, nor do we know whether he was indeed canonized. He falls into the category of locally venerated saints (see * E. Golubinsky, *The History of the Canonization of Saints in the Russian Church*, Moscow, 1903, p. 340). His depiction is encountered only in very late icons. The earliest writers to mention him include Joseph Volotsky (see * J. Volotsky, *The Great Martyrologies Assembled by the Metropolitan Macarius of All Russia*, St Petersburg, 1870, October 1—13, pp. 26, 27). The present scene reflects a reality gleaned from written records that tell of St Sabbatheus's sojourn on a desolate bank of the River Orsha, the cave that he 'dug' and the venerated cross. The depiction is commented on in an extensive inscription. The overall presentation is consonant with the traditional manner employed in sixteenth-century Russian painting to depict ascetic exploits.

Provenance: In the eighteenth and nineteenth centuries the icon was in the Cathedral of the Presentation in the Temple of the St Sabbatheus Monastery which was abolished in 1764. Its later history is unknown. It entered the Rublev Museum in 1971.

Exhibitions: 1978 Moscow

References: * A. Mitropolsky, *Outline of the History of the St Sabbatheus Monastery, now the Village of Savvatyevo, in the Tver District, Prefaced by a Biography of the Monastery's Founder Sabbatheus, Ascetic of Tver and Orsha*, Tver, 1897, pp. 33, 64, 74, 107, 108, 112, 114, 116, 117, 120—123; Sergeyev 1977, p. 263, ill. between p. 256 and p. 257; * V. N. Sergeyev, "St Sabbatheus of Orsha. 16th Century. Tver", in: *Father's Home*, Moscow, 1978, pp. 78—81, ill. p. 77; Popov 1979, pp. 230, 231, 327, 345, 346, ill. p. 461; Saltykov 1981, pp. 39, 40 (note 38), 58, 246, 247, ill. 78

137—139. ST ANASTASIA, ST NICHOLAS AND THE APOSTLE JAMES
First half of the 16th century
111×87
Tretyakov Gallery, Moscow
Inv. No. 15027

State of preservation: Good on the whole with minor losses of priming. The part of the icon, which was obscured by a time-darkened varnish of linseed oil and insignificant overpainting when it entered the Tretyakov Gallery, was cleaned by E. A. Malkina in 1976—86.

Iconography: The work belongs to the type of icon with selected saints that was common in fifteenth- and sixteenth-century Russian, especially Novgorodian, painting. As a rule they included the highly revered saints, such as St Nicholas (see Cat. Nos. 12—14; 87, 88), St Anastasia, like St Parasceve (Cat. Nos. 129—133), is a kind of collective image, as legends tell of several martyrs of that name (for more detail see Popov 1979, pp. 328, 329; Smirnova, Laurina, Gordiyenko 1982, pp. 240, 241).

St James is one of two of that name among the Twelve Apostles, whose feast-days are October 9/22 and April 30/May 13 (see Sergius 1876, part 1, pp. 111, 268, 269; * *The Theological Encyclopedia of the Orthodox Church*, edited by N. D. Lopukhin, Petrograd, vol. 6, pp. 55—91). The way in which he is depicted, in chiton and himation, and holding a scroll in his left hand, is likewise quite traditional.

Provenance: From the collection of A. Anisimov. Entered the Tretyakov Gallery in 1931 (see also Cat. Nos. 6, 7; 8, 9; 69—86).

References: Antonova, Mneva 1963, I, No. 310, pp. 362, 363; Popov 1979, pp. 182, 221, 222, 227, 327—329, ills. pp. 223, 446; Ryndina 1979, p. 535; Smirnova, Laurina, Gordiyenko 1982, pp. 240, 281

140—157. ST IPATIOS OF GANGRA WITH SCENES FROM HIS LIFE
16th century
112×81
Tretyakov Gallery, Moscow
Inv. No. 6135

State of preservation: On the whole good with insertions of priming and minor damages on marginal scenes Nos. 1, 9, 11 and 16. Inscriptions have suffered most and some losses have been tinted by a 'neutral' brown tempera.

Iconography: According to legend St Ipatios was Bishop of Gangra, the centre of the Byzantine province of Paphlagonia on the southern shore of the Black Sea. He was martyred and died *ca.* 321 or 336 (his feast-day is March 31/April 13) during the reign of the Emperor Constantine I the Great. He is said to have been killed by the enemies of Christianity, by that time the official religion. The text of his Life (Martyrdom) upon which the marginal scenes are based, is apocryphal and has been recorded in Russian at least since the late fifteenth century (see * *The Russian History Library*, St Petersburg, 1908, vol. 6, p. 792, and also * N. Tikhonravov, *Works of Prohibited Russian Literature*, vol. 2, Moscow, 1863, pp. 121—145). St Ipatios was venerated as an opponent of the Arian heresy and diabolical powers; illustrations of his hagiography can be found as early as the tenth century in works of illumination (Vat. gr. 1613— *The*

Menology of Basil II; * S. Der-Ner-sesian, "Muscovite Menology", in: *Byzantium. The Southern Slavs and Ancient Rus. Western Europe*, Moscow, 1973, p. 101). The figure portrayed in the centre is typical of depictions of bishops. The marginal scenes — which run horizontally from left to right in a order incorrect when compared to the text of the Martyrdom — are as follows: 1) St Ipatios preaching to the clergy in Gangra; 2) Soldiers are ordered by the hegemon (no doubt the ruler of the province, later sometimes referred to in the text as king) to arrest St Ipatios; 3) St Ipatios converses with the hegemon-king; 4) St Ipatios baptizes the hegemon; 5) St Ipatios resurrects the hegemon's wife; 6) St Ipatios is roasted alive (his first death); 7) St Ipatios vanquishes with his cross, or wand, the serpent from the sea that has taken over the palace; 8) St Ipatios is roasted alive inside a brazen bull (his sixth death); 9) St Ipatios is dashed to death against rocks by a horse (his second death); 10) The Devil in the shape of an angel appears to St Ipatios in the dungeon; 11) St Ipatios is pressed beneath a stone and has molten tin poured down his throat; 12) Christ appears to St Ipatios in the dungeon (which may

have preceded the tortures, and should therefore be before the bishop's several deaths); 13) St Ipatios is boiled 'piecemeal' in a cauldron (his third death); 14) St Ipatios has his arms and legs lopped off; 15) St Ipatios converses with some hegemon (it is impossible to say exactly with whom and when due to the confused arrangement of the scenes); 16) St Ipatios is cast into a pit and buried under rocks (his seventh death).

Provenance: Unknown. Entered the Tretyakov Gallery in 1924—25 from the State Museum Reserve.

Exhibitions: 1958 Moscow; 1969—70 Moscow; 1975 Moscow

References: Alpatow 1958, p. 26, ill. 7; Antonova, Mneva 1963, I, No. 204, pp. 238, 239, pls. 147, 148; Tver Painting 1970, p. 25 (No. 18); Popov 1970, pp. 317, 328, 329, ill. p. 321; Seventh Exhibition 1975, p. 27; Smirnova 1976, p. 163, note 23; Popov 1979, pp. 182, 221—227, 329—333, ills. pp. 224, 225, 447—451; Lazarev 1983, pp. 130, 503

158. ROYAL DOORS. SCENES: THE ANNUNCIATION; THE EVANGELIST JOHN AND ST PROCHORUS; THE EVANGELIST MATTHEW
Middle or third quarter of the 16th century
137×36
Museum of History and Art, Sergiyev Posad
Inv. No. 7171

State of preservation: Good on the whole with losses greatest on the margins and background and with considerable insertion of priming on the figure of St Prochorus in the central scene. Also much crackling.

Iconography: Traditional (see Cat. Nos. 104, 105 and, for later analogies, Popov 1979, p. 356). The texts on the scrolls correspond to the opening passages of the Gospels according to SS John and Matthew.

Provenance: From the Tver Church of the White Trinity. Entered the Zagorsk (now Sergiyev Posad) Museum in 1960. The leaf's previous history is obscure, as it could have been transferred to the church after the revolution; no precise archival evidence has been found. Pre-revolu-

tionary writers repeatedly mention old Trinity Doors, but no definite identification of these with the surviving leaf has yet been made.

Exhibitions: 1966 Leningrad; 1969—70 Moscow; 1975 Moscow

References: Vladislavlev 1863, p. 113; Zhiznevsky 1888, p. 62; Nekrasov 1900, p. 17; * *Early Russian Art Exhibition: Results of Russian Federation Museum Expeditions to Locate and Collect Works of Early Russian Art. Catalogue*, Leningrad, 1966, p. 24; Sixth Exhibition 1969, p. 81; S. Yamshchikov, *Old Russian Painting. New Discoveries* (in Russian and English), Leningrad, 1969, 2nd ed., pl. 32; Tver Painting 1970, p. 34 (No. 35); Seventh Exhibition 1975, p. 28; Popov 1979, pp. 316, 320, 355, 356, ill. p. 465

159—161. ST NICHOLAS WITH SCENES FROM HIS LIFE
Ca. 1560s
64×40.5
Tver Picture Gallery
Inv. No. Ж-1237

State of preservation: Poor on the whole. Traces of repeated repairs and reworking of the mounting over the entire surface with the centre as well as the right-hand vertical row of marginal scenes and the margins heavily damaged. Numerous heavy touchings up.

Iconography: The figure in the centre is traditional and of a type popular in Russian painting since the fourteenth century. The biographical cycle of the saint is likewise among the oldest in Russian painting (Smirnova 1976, pp. 184—187, 199—203).

The variant given in the present icon was an established one for its time. A whole series of similar icons of the same size and the same set of border scenes — with minor variations — were produced in the first half and middle of the sixteenth century. The border scenes should be followed in a manner similar to Cat. Nos. 129—133 with regard to the scenes along the vertical edges — apparently they share a single prototype. The scenes depict: 1) Birth of St Nicholas; 2) Baptism; 3) Novitiate; 4) Ordination as Deacon; 5) Ordination as Bishop by the Metropolitan; 6) The cleaving of the tree, combined with the exorcising of a 'treasure-spring'; 7) The miraculous rescue of the seamen, one of several similar hagiographical episodes; 8) The appearance of St Nicholas to the king (Emperor Constantine), in a dream, which introduces the story of the three warriors or stratilates; 9) St Nicholas visits the three men in their dungeon; 10) St Nicholas saves the three men from the sword; 11) St Nicholas saves Demetrius, who venerated the saint and set off from Constantinople to Atira to attend celebrations of his feast-day; 12) St Nicholas returns Basil, son of a peasant from the shores of Lycia who had been captured by the Saracens, to the arms of his parents; 13) The burial of St Nicholas; 14) The transfer of the coffin with the relics of St Nicholas from Myra in Lycia to Bari in Italy, where they remain to this day.

Provenance: From the Tver Church of the White Trinity, probably from the Chapel of St Nicholas. Entered the Kalinin Gallery in 1949. During restoration in 1966—69, a chronicle inscription from 1826 was removed from beneath the saint's feet in the centrepiece. It was similar to that preserved on the Trinity icon of identical provenance (Cat. Nos. 119, 120), and also reported that the icon had been 'conceived' by Nechai in 1561. In this particular case, the date corresponds more closely to the style. No information has been discovered on the identity of the person who commissioned the icon, though he may have been of the Lamin or Tushinsky merchant family, which founded the church (for more detail see Popov 1979, pp. 348, 349).

Exhibitions: 1969—70 Moscow

References: Vladislavlev 1863, p. 114; Nekrasov 1900, p. 13; Pogozheva 1914, p. 43; Tver Painting 1970, p. 33 (No. 34); Popov 1979, pp. 215, 231, 232, 347—349, ill. p. 462

162. THE MIRACLE OF ST GEORGE AND THE DRAGON
**Second half of the 16th century.
By a Tver provincial artist**

99×79
Tretyakov Gallery, Moscow
Inv. No. 13888

State of preservation: Good on the whole. Losses and insertions of priming in the margins and also in the bottom right-hand corner.

Iconography: Represents a well-developed compositional version that was established by the sixteenth century. In Russian painting the oldest representation of the theme is found in the twelfth-century frescoes of the Church of St George in Staraya Ladoga. From the fourteenth century on, the subject acquired exceptional popularity, gradually growing more complex and including additional narrative detail (for the legendary sources of the Miracle and its iconography see: * A. Kirpichnikov, *St George and Yegory the Brave*, St Petersburg, 1879; * A. V. Rystenko, "The Legend of St George and the Dragon in Byzantine and Slavo-Russian Literatures", *Transactions of Novorossiysk University*, Odessa, 1909, issue 112; Lazarev 1970, pp. 94—98; Smirnova 1976, pp. 189—192; see also Cat. No. 84).

Provenance: From the Kashin Cathedral of the Resurrection. Sent to the Central Restoration Workshops in the 1920s, after which it entered the Historical Museum in Moscow and subsequently the Tretyakov Gallery in 1930. Stylistically close to Cat. No. 172.

Exhibitions: 1926 Moscow; 1969—70 Moscow

References: A. Anisimov, *Guide to the Exhibition of Old Russian Icon-* *Painting in the Historical Museum*, Moscow, 1926, p. 27, No. 206; Antonova, Mneva 1963, I, p. 243, No. 208; Tver Painting 1970, p. 30, No. 26; Popov 1979, pp. 240, 241, 354, ill. p. 238

163—168. THE NATIVITY OF THE VIRGIN WITH SCENES FROM HER LIFE
Third quarter of the 16th century. By a Tver artist (?)
139×111

Rublev Museum of Early Russian Art, Moscow

Inv. No. КП 427

State of preservation: Good on the whole with minor losses of priming and abrasions of the paint layer. Touching up approximates to the original colours of the painting.

Iconography: The centrepiece presents a more complex version of the composition, with the story unfolding from the Annunciation to St Joachim and St Anne to the Caressing of the Virgin in the upper tier. Similar representations are characteristic of painting in the middle and second half of the sixteenth century and are not confined to the Mariological theme. Small icons on the same theme with a similar iconography can be found in the collections of the Sergiyev Posad (formerly Zagorsk) Museum and the Tretyakov Gallery (see * T. N. Manushina, *Zagorsk. Old Russian Painting in the Collection of the Zagorsk Museum of History and Art*, Moscow, 1976, p. 49; * N. E. Mneva, "Muscovite Painting of the 16th Century", in: *The History of Russian Art*, Moscow, 1955, vol. 3, ill. p. 581; see also Cat. Nos. 15; 20—22). Iconographically, the border scenes, incorporating the Protevangelical story of SS Joachim and Anne and the Virgin's childhood as well as the Gospel period of her life, follow established tradition (for which see Lafontaine-Dosogne 1975, pp. 163—194). In Russian monumental painting the Protevangelical scenes first appeared in the eleventh-century wall-paintings in the Kiev Cathedral of St Sophia and they became relatively common in the fourteenth century, as, for instance, in the frescoes (1313) of the Cathedral of the Nativity of the Snetogorsk Monastery near Pskov, and also later, as in the frescoes (1360s—80s) of the Church of the Dormition-on-the-Volotovo-Field near Novgorod. In icon-painting the theme was taken

up in later works such as the late fifteenth-century hagiographical icon of the Virgin of Tikhvin from Novgorod, although painted by a Muscovite artist (see * V. Gippenreiter, E. Gordiyenko, S. Yamshchikov, *Novgorod*, Moscow, 1971). The present icon follows the same iconographical tradition. The border scenes run from top to bottom, left to right as follows: 1) St Joachim and St Anne bearing gifts; 2) The high priest rejects the gifts; 3) The Annunciation to St Joachim; 4) The Annunciation to St Anne; 5) St Joachim and St Anne meet at the Golden Gates (conception of the Virgin); 6) The Infant Virgin is presented to the high priest to be named; 7) The first seven steps of the Virgin; 8) Her presentation in the temple; 9) Praying for the staffs; 10) Zacharias gives the Virgin in marriage to St Joseph; 11) The Annunciation by the well; 12) The Virgin prays in the wilderness; 13) The Annunciation of the Dormition; 14) The preparation for the Dormition; 15) The Dormition of the Virgin; 16) The Assumption of the Virgin.

Provenance: From the Church of the Nativity of the Virgin in Isayevets. Entered the Kalinin Museum between 1929 and 1935, and in 1962 was transferred to the Rublev Museum. Isayevets, formerly a village just outside Tver, was owned by the Pleshcheyev family in the sixteenth century, but was later apparently acquired by Boris Godunov (Vladislavlev 1863, p. 118).

Exhibitions: 1969—70 Moscow

References: Tver Painting 1970, p. 35 (No. 37); Popov 1979, pp. 11, 235—237, ill. p. 233

169. PORTABLE ICONOSTASIS
Third quarter of the 16th century
(by a Pskov artist)

64×98
Tver Picture Gallery
Inv. No. Ж-1239

State of preservation: Good on the whole, with partial losses in the margins, minor damage and abrasion. The numerous inscriptions have suffered most damage.

Iconography: An abbreviated iconostasis. In the fifteenth century similar embroidered iconostases were confined to the representations of the Deesis tier. Only one extant example of early vintage, commissioned in 1466 by Prince Mikhail Andreyevich of Vereya and his wife, presents a multi-tiered version incorporating several of the figures who feature in the frescoes embellishing chancel screens (in the Astrakhan Museum of Local Lore; see * T. V. Nikolayeva, *Works of Russian Applied Art with Inscriptions of the 15th and First Quarter of the 16th Century*, Moscow, 1971, No. 37). In the late sixteenth century and seventeenth century painted folding iconostases were no longer rare. However, they lack the tier that would correspond to the chancel screens and in this respect the portable iconostasis adheres, as far as we can judge, to the earlier tradition. The selection of scenes and figures comprise a freely arranged, yet structurally and symbolically strict version of the normal iconostasis. The scenes and figures represented are arranged in tiers from left to right as follows: first tier — 1) The Nativity of the Virgin; 2) The Annunciation; 3) The Nativity of Christ; 4) The Baptism; 5) The Transfiguration; 6) The Ascension; 7) The Dormition; second tier — the Deesis with the Apostle Thomas, the Apostle Matthew, St John the Divine, the Apostle Peter, the Archangel Michael, the Virgin, Christ in Majesty, St John the Baptist, the Archangel Gabriel, the Apostle Paul, the Apostle Mark, the Apostle Luke and the Apostle Philip; third tier — 1) The warrior saints Panteleimon, Eustace, Christopher, Nicetas, George and Menas; 2) The sainted princes Dovmont, Vsevolod-Gabriel, Princess Olga, Boris, Vladimir and Gleb; 3) The Harrowing of Hell; 4) The Bishops and Metropolitans Nicholas, Isaiah, Leontius and John of Rostov, and Peter and Alexius of Moscow; 5) The Old Testament Trinity (the Hospitality of Abraham); 6) The warrior saints and healers Andrew Stratilates, Cosmas, Damian, Florus, Demetrius of the Thessalonica and Laurus; 7) The female martyrs Juliana, Photinia, Maura, Parasceve Piatnitsa, Catherine and Anastasia; fourth, bottom tier — the holy saints Macarius of Rome (or of Egypt), Onuphrius the Great, Peter of Athos, Mark of Thrace, Alexander of Svir, Zosimus and Sabbatheus of Solovki, Demetrius of Prilutsk (inscribed 'of Vologda'), Macarius of Kaliazin, Cyril of Belozersk, Sergius of Radonezh. Euthymius the Great, Stephen the Younger, Pachomius the Great, Ephraim the Syrian, Anthony and Theodoseus of the Caves, John Archbishop of Novgorod, Barlaam of Khutyn, Joasaphus Prince of India and Barlaam the Ascetic, Euphrosyne of Pskov, Maximus the Blessed and Basil the Blessed of Moscow, Andrew Salus and Mary of Egypt. In the sixteenth century this was the most extensive gallery of 'portraits' of Russian princes and church hierarchs. Typical too is the ascetic aspect, with the hermit and monk clearly dominant.

Provenance: In the nineteenth and early twentieth centuries this work was kept in the Tver Church of the White Trinity from which it entered the Kalinin Gallery in 1949. Originally it may have been in the Cathedral of the Transfiguration of Our Saviour and have been commissioned by the local Pskov-born Bishop Sabbatheus (1570—1572 or 1573); see the introduction. That the painter was definitely from Pskov is indicated, apart from the style and many Pskovian saints, by the inclusion among the sainted Russian princes of Dovmont (died 1299), who was officially canonized no earlier than the close of the sixteenth century (see * V. I. Okhotnikova, *The Tale of Dovmont*, Leningrad, 1985, pp. 159, 160). This circumstance makes it difficult to precisely date the icon, as it is almost impossible that it was painted at the end of the sixteenth century or after the canonization of

St Basil the Blessed in 1588. The style appears unexpectedly archaic, which conflicts with the icon's patently pro-Muscovite artistic tendencies. Still, we may note that from the middle of the century the portrayal of locally venerated Russian saints was not that rare, as is illustrated by the frescoes in the Moscow Kremlin Cathedral of the Annunciation (1547—1551).

References: Nekrasov 1900, pp. 14—16; * *The Minutes of the Sittings of the Board of the Historico-Archaeological Committee of the Tver Eparchy for 1903—04*, Tver, 1904, p. 8 (presenting a summary of V. I. Nekrasov's communication); * V. I. Antonova, "Easel Painting of Medieval Russia", in: *Three Centuries of Art*, Moscow, 1976, pp. 188—194, ills. pp. 186, 188; Popov 1979, pp. 236, 237, 309, ill. p. 235; * M. V. Alpatov. I. S. Rodnikova, *Pskov Icons: 13th to 16th Centuries*, Leningrad, 1990, pp. 316, 317, Cat. No. 148

170, 171. ST NICHOLAS WITH CHRIST AND THE VIRGIN
Third quarter of the 16th century
100×78
Tver Picture Gallery
Inv. No. Ж-1119

State of preservation: Affected by numerous renovations. Major losses and abrasions, with insertions of seventeenth- and eighteenth-century priming below. Considerable touching up, with the lettering of the Gospel text additionally painted in.

Iconography: Traditional (see Cat. Nos. 87, 88), with, however, such a relatively rare detail as the Gospel open at the reading (Luke VI, 17) for the service on the saint's day.

Provenance: From the Tver Church of St Nicholas in the Volhynia Quarter, where it had been in the southern narthex before entering the Kalinin Gallery in 1939. The church is known to have existed from the mid-sixteenth century (* I. I. Lappo, *The Tver Uyezd in the 16th Century*, Moscow, 1894, p. 188).

Exhibitions: 1969—70 Moscow

References: Tver Painting 1970, p. 32, No. 32; Popov 1979, pp. 234, 354, 361—369, ills. pp. 472, 473

172. THE VERNICLE. CHRIST ENTOMBED ('KING OF GLORY')
Second half of the 16th century

134.5×87.5
Hermitage, St Petersburg
Inv. No. Э/ри-489

State of preservation: Good on the whole with minor losses of painting in the margins and abrasions of the paint layer.

Iconography: Both subjects are quite common in Balkan and Russian painting. The Vernicle, known in Russian as The Holy Image of Our Saviour Unwrought by Human Hand, was first depicted in Russian icons in the twelfth century (Porfiryev 1890, pp. 239—270, 276—281; Kondakov 1905, pp. 14—18; * A. N. Grabar, *The Vernicle of the Lansky Cathedral*, Prague, 1930; * G. I. Vzdornov, "The Icon of the Vernicle, a Monument of 15th-Century Pskovian Painting', in: *Sovietskaya arkheologiya* (Soviet Archaeology), 1973, No. 3, pp. 214, 215). The presentation of *Christ Entombed*, or the *King in Glory* or *Do not mourn for me, Mother* (*Pietà*) gained popularity from the end of the fourteenth century, a period which saw a powerful tide of Balkan influences (Lazarev 1970, pp. 277, 278; for a review of iconographic variants see: T. Dobrzeniecki, "Imago Pietatis. Its Meaning and Function", *Bulletin du Museé National de Varsovie*, 1971, XII, No. 1—2, pp. 5—27). The Vernicle shown either on cloth or on tile was imbued with the distinct character of a protective talisman. On the other hand the subject of the Christ entombed is definitely ascetic in nature, part of the Passion. The combination of the two on one icon is extremely rare; the only other known example is a fourteenth- or fifteenth-century icon from North Russia which is now in the Arkhangelsk Art Museum. In Tver, however, this was not the only icon of its kind and this is evidence of some particular local cult. A double-sided icon may possibly have been the source of such works.

Provenance: From the Kashin Cathedral of the Resurrection. Entered the Hermitage in 1961. As this icon is known to have undergone restoration at the hands of P. I. Yukin in the 1920s, it is interesting to note in this connection that documents

mention several icons on the same
subject. It is by no means impossible
that the icon here had been in the
Tver Cathedral of the Ascension or in
its chapel of the Holy Image (the
Vernicle) and came into the Kashin
Cathedral much later.

References: Popov 1979, pp. 14, 240,
241, 270, 354, ill. p. 238; Smirnova,
Laurina, Gordiyenko 1982, p. 345

173. DOOR TO A PROTHESIS. SCENES: THE EXPULSION FROM PARADISE; THE PARABLE OF THE LAME MAN AND THE BLIND MAN
First half of the 17th century
97×58
Tver Picture Gallery
Inv. No. Ж-1125

State of preservation: Good on the
whole, with minor losses and touching
up.
Iconography: Of the several themes
depicted on side altar doors in the
sixteenth and seventeenth centuries
(cf. Cat. Nos. 85, 86) the story of
Adam and Eve the depiction of the
Garden of Eden as well as various
scenes of a didactic nature are
commonest (for more detail see

* V. N. Sergeyev, "The Ecclesiastic
Poem of the Grief of Adam on an
Icon", *Transactions of the Department
of Old Russian Literature*, Leningrad,
1971, vol. XXVI).

Provenance: From the Old-Believer
Church of the Dormition in Tver.
Entered the Kalinin Gallery in 1947.

174, 175. THE VIRGIN OF THE SIGN, AND ST NICHOLAS WITH CHRIST AND THE VIRGIN
A double-sided icon. Last quarter of the 16th or early 17th century
47.5×41 (handle — 92 cm long)
Tver Picture Gallery
Inv. No. Ж-1236

State of preservation: Good on the
whole, except for the sphere enclosing
the Infant Christ, with minor losses
and abrasions of the paint layer and
touching up.
Iconography: The combination of the
Holy Virgin and Child with St Nicholas
is an established tradition for processional icons (see Cat. Nos. 12—14;
15; 87, 88). Though the Virgin of the
Sign is not that frequent a variant,
it is by far the most popular schema
on such icons, which is due to a
particular legend about the Battle
between the Men of Novgorod and the
Men of Suzdal in 1170 (for more
detail see Smirnova, Laurina,
Gordiyenko 1982, pp. 218, 219; for
the bibliography of the oldest such icon
see: *Painting of Pre-Mongol Russia.
Exhibition Catalogue*, compiled by
S. A. Korina, Moscow, 1974, pp. 51—
54). One exceptional iconographic
feature of the icon's obverse is the
seated figure of Christ Emmanuel

in the sphere, which may derive
from early sources (see Popov 1979,
pp. 364, 365). For the Gospel text on
the book that St Nicholas holds —
cf. Cat. Nos. 170, 171.

Provenance: From the Tver Church
of the White Trinity. Entered the
Kalinin Gallery in 1949. May have
been earlier in the Volhynia Quarter
cemetery church (Cat. Nos. 170,
171).

References: Popov 1979, pp. 14, 234,
363—365, ill. pp. 474, 475

176, 177. THE NATIVITY OF THE VIRGIN
First half of the 17th century. By a Volga Region artist

107×78

Rublev Museum of Early Russian Art, Moscow

Inv. No. КП 273

State of preservation: Good.

Iconography: Belongs to the established version of the composition that was completely traditional for the second half of the sixteenth century and the seventeenth century (see Cat. Nos. 15; 20—22). The representation of geese at a spring is an image that derives from the report of St Anne's lamentation at the moment of the Annunciation to her of the birth of the Virgin (Cat. Nos. 163—168).

Provenance: From the village of Driutskovo near Bezhetsk in the neighbourhood of Tver. Entered the Rublev Museum in 1965.

Exhibitions: 1970 Canada; 1972 Novosibirsk; 1973—74 Moscow

References: Vagner, Kukles, Tikhomirova 1972, p. 102, ill. 26; Saltykov 1981, pp. 51, 52, 251, ill. 177

178, 179. ST NICHOLAS WITH SCENES FROM HIS LIFE
Second half of the 17th century. By a Volga Region artist

95.5×68.5

Rublev Museum of Early Russian Art, Moscow

Inv. No. КП 310

State of preservation: Good, with minor damage.

Iconography: Traditional (see Cat. Nos. 159—161). The border scenes are arranged with the right-hand scene beneath the last of the upper tier coming after it, followed by the column of scenes on the left-hand side. They depict: 1) The birth of St Nicholas; 2) His baptism; 3) St Nicholas declines to suck at his mother's breast on fast days; 4) Novitiate; 5) Ordination as deacon; 6) Ordination as bishop (archbishop); 7) His appearance to the Emperor Constantine in a dream; 8) His appearance to the three officers in the dungeon; 9) The exorcising of the spring; 10) The saving of the shipwrecked sailors from drowning; 11) The saving of Demetrius; 12) The returning of Basil, son of Agricus, to his parents; 13) The dormition of St Nicholas; 14) The translation of the relics of St Nicholas from Myra in Lycia to Bari.

Provenance: From the village of Spasskoye-on-the Nerl near Kaliazin in the neighbourhood of Tver. Entered the Rublev Museum in 1965.

Exhibitions: 1977 Leningrad

References: *17th- and 18th-Century Russian Painting from the Russian and Rublev Museums and the Tretyakov Gallery. Exhibition Catalogue*, Leningrad, 1971, pp. 76, 77, ill.; Saltykov 1981, p. 252, ills. 187, 188

180, 181. PRINCE MIKHAIL YAROSLAVICH AND XENIA OF TVER
Late 17th century

51×40

Rublev Museum of Early Russian Art, Moscow

Inv. No. ВП 526

State of preservation: Good, with a contemparary silver mounting.

Iconography: Belongs to the type of donor or church-warden portrait that was fairly widely known in Byzantine art. In Russian painting and book illumination such portraits appeared in the eleventh century, but did not become as common as in the Balkans. Indeed, in Russian painting donor compositions were rather exceptional. Though the specific historical portrait had become popular in Muscovite art by the time this icon was painted, its spatial concept was different (cf. Cat. No. 182). The icon here is representative of the earlier stage — which is precisely a donor portrayal — whose salient feature is the inclusion of the model of a city or church. In the present icon Mikhail and Xenia (who changed her name to Maria when she took holy vows, as an inscription on the silver mounting informs us) appear as the first major builders of Tver and the founders, in 1285—90, of its Cathedral of the Transfiguration. In the centre of the model in the foreground we see the city's Vladimir Gate and behind it on the left-hand side the Cathedral and the Church of the Annunciation. In the middle behind the tower, the bell-tower, and on the right what is most likely the Monastery of St Athanasius, behind which are the Prince's Palace with two royal churches of the Archangel Michael and of SS Boris and Gleb. The entire ensemble apparently shows Tver as it looked in the fifteenth century during the reign of Boris Alexandrovich — as V. A. Meniaylo tells us in his special paper devoted to the icon. This is evidence of a particular tradition of portraiture which derives from the frontispiece miniature of the *Chronicle of Georgius Hamartolos* (ill. 4).

Provenance: From the sacristy of the Tver Cathedral of the Transfiguration where it was deposited in 1702 by Archbishop Sergius (1682—1702). Though known to scholars in the 1860s, it subsequently disappeared from view until it was eventually acquired by the Rublev Museum from a private individual in 1984. This icon, reproduced in A. Sokolov's publication of 1864, was taken as a point of departure for scholars studying the history of early Russian architecture, who followed pre-revolutionary writers in believing the icon to have been from the fifteenth century. We now have documentary evidence of a series of similar donor portraits in the seventeenth century.

References: * A. Sokolov, *The Sainted Pious Grand Prince Mikhail Yaroslavich of Tver*, Tver, 1864, lithographed frontispiece; * E. A. Rikman, "New Materials on the Topography of Early Tver", *Brief Transactions of the Institute of the History of Material Culture*, Moscow, 1953, issue 49, pp. 40—44; N. N. Voronin, *North-Eastern Russian Architecture of the 12th—15th Centuries*, vol. 2, Moscow, 1962, pp. 140, 390—398, figs. 75, 193; V. A. Kuchkin, *The Tales of Mikhail of Tver*, Moscow, 1974, p. 167; Popov 1979, pp. 21, 98, 346

182. BISHOP ARSENIUS AND PRINCE MIKHAIL YAROSLAVICH OF TVER
Late 17th century
30.5×27
Tver Picture Gallery
Inv. No. Ж-860

State of preservation: Good, with minor abrasions and tinted losses through collector's restoration.

Iconography: Typologically similar to Cat. Nos. 180, 181. However, now both the spatial concept and the sense are different. These are already portraits of sainted historical figures against a definite landscape — the scene of their lives and activities. A number of similar icons can be found depicting the Moscow Metropolitans Peter and Alexius against the background of the Kremlin, painted in the Armoury between the 1660s and the 1690s (Antonova, Mneva 1963, 2, p. 384, ill. 181). First to produce this type of portrait was Simon Ushakov with his 1668 icon of the *Tree of the State of Muscovy. Acathistos to the Virgin of Vladimir*, in which we see the fourteenth-century founding fathers of Muscovy symbolically attending on the Tsar Alexei Mikhailovich against the background of the Kremlin towers as rebuilt in the seventeenth century and the Cathedral of the Dormition (Antonova, Mneva 1963, vol. 2, p. 384, ills. 142, 143). We may similarly construe our icon's scenic representation of central Tver. Despite the external verisimilitude, a conventional, decorative treatment of the architecture predominates. Icons of this type may have been painted following the canonization of Bishop Arsenius in 1483 (* E. Golubinsky, *The History of the Canonization of Saints in the Russian Church*, Moscow, 1903, pp. 18—30). However, the present icon's dependence on an early source is limited to the overall iconographic scheme. This piece is already representative of the transitional style (cf. pl. 36).

Provenance: Entered the Tver Museum in 1893 from the well-known collector P. I. Shchukin. Transferred to the Kalinin Gallery from the Kalinin Museum of Local Lore in 1937.

References: Popov 1979, pp. 98, 346

KEY TO ABBREVIATIONS

EXHIBITIONS

1913 MOSCOW
Exhibition of Early Russian Art. Moscow, Institute of Archaeology, 1913

1920 MOSCOW
Second Exhibition of the Central Restoration Workshops. Moscow, the Higher Artistic and Industrial Workshops (VKhUTEMAS), 1920

1921 SERGIYEV
Exhibition of Early Russian Art in the Museum of the Former Trinity-St Sergius Monastery, Sergiyev, 1921

1926 MOSCOW
Exhibition of Works of Early Russian Icon-Painting. Moscow, Historical Museum, 1926

1929—32 GERMANY, ENGLAND, AUSTRIA, USA
Exhibition of Works of Early Russian Painting in Germany, England, Austria and the USA, Sponsored by the People's Commissariat of Education of the Russian Federation, 1929—32

1957 WARSAW
Russian Painting. 14th—20th Centuries. Warsaw, National Museum, 1957

1958 MOSCOW
Exhibition of Icons Marking the Fourth International Convention of Slavists. Moscow, Tretyakov Gallery, 1958

1959 LONDON
Russian Painting from the 13th to the 20th Centuries. London, 1959

1960 MOSCOW
Andrei Rublev Exhibition, Commemorating the 600th Anniversary of the Birth of the Great Early Russian Artist. Moscow, Tretyakov Gallery, 1960

1964 MOSCOW
Exhibition of Russian Wooden Sculpture and Decorative Carving. Moscow. Exhibition Hall of the Moscow Branch of the Artists' Union of the Russian Federation, 1964

1966 LENINGRAD
Results of Russian Federation Museum Expeditions to Locate and Collect Works of Early Russian Art. Leningrad, Russian Museum, 1966

1967 ARCHAEOLOGY
Archaeology of the USSR. Holland, Switzerland, Federal Republic of Germany and Italy, 1967

1967 MOSCOW
Sixth Exhibition of Works of Fine Art Restored by the Grabar Workshops. Moscow, USSR Academy of Arts, 1967

1967 MOSCOW, TRETYAKOV GALLERY
The Rostov-Suzdalian School of Painting. Moscow, Tretyakov Gallery, 1967

1967—68 PARIS
Russian Art from the Scythians to the Present. Treasures from Soviet Museums. Paris, Grand Palais, 1967—68

1968 MOSCOW
New Discoveries and Acquisitions of the Tretyakov Gallery and Rublev Museum. Moscow, Rublev Museum, 1968

1969 MOSCOW
Exhibition of New Acquisitions. 1963—1968. Moscow, Tretyakov Gallery, 1969

1969—70 MOSCOW
Painting of Ancient Tver. Moscow, Andrei Rublev Museum of Early Russian Art, 1969—70

1970 CANADA
Expo-70. Canada, Montreal, 1970

1972 MOSCOW
Painting of Medieval Russia and the Balkans. Moscow, Rublev Museum, 1972

1972 NOVOSIBIRSK
Early Russian Painting. 16th—17th Centuries. Novosibirsk, 1972

1973 BUDAPEST
Works of Early Russian Painting. Budapest, 1973

1973—74 MOSCOW
Early Russian Painting from the Tretyakov Gallery Collection. Moscow, Arkhangelskoye Estate Museum, 1973—74

1974 HELSINKI
Early Russian Art. 900—1600. Helsinki, 1974

1975 MOSCOW
Seventh Exhibition of Works of Fine Art Restored by the Grabar Workshops (1944—74). Moscow, USSR Academy of Arts, 1975

1976 LENINGRAD
Dionysius and Muscovite Art. 15th—16th Centuries. Leningrad, Russian Museum, 1976

1977 LENINGRAD
Russian Painting. 17th—18th Centuries. Leningrad, Russian Museum, 1977

1978 MOSCOW
New Discoveries and Acquisitions of the Rublev Museum. Moscow, Rublev Museum, 1978

1983 MOSCOW
Restoration of Museum Treasures in the USSR. Moscow, Central Exhibition Hall of the Artists Union of the USSR, 1983

REFERENCES
Russian sources

ANTONOVA, MNEVA 1963
V. I. Antonova, N. E. Mneva, *The State Tretyakov Gallery. Catalogue of Early Russian Painting. An Attempt at Historical and Artistic Classification*, Moscow, 1963, vols. 1 and 2

BRIUSOVA 1974
V. G. Briusova, "Nilus the Greek, Bishop of Tver, and His Epistle to Prince Georgi Ivanovich", *Transactions of the Department of Early Russian Literature of the USSR Academy of Sciences Institute of Russian Literature*, Moscow—Leningrad, 1974, vol. 28

DIONYSIUS 1981
Dionysius and Muscovite Art of the 15th—16th Centuries. The State Russian Museum. Exhibition Catalogue, introduction by V. K. Laurina, selection and editing by T. B. Vilinbakhova, V. K. Laurina and G. D. Petrova, Leningrad, 1981

DMITRIYEV 1940
Yu. U. Dmitriyev, *A Guide to the State Russian Museum. Early Russian Art*, Leningrad—Moscow, 1940

GOLUBEV 1979
S. I. Golubev, "Concerning the Origin of the Kashin Iconostasis", in: G. V. Popov, A. V. Ryndina, *Painting and Applied Art. 14th—16th Centuries*, Moscow, 1979, appendix, pp. 366—368

GRABAR 1926 (IDEM 1966)
I. E. Grabar, "Andrei Rublev. An Outline of His Work on the Basis of Restorations Carried Out in 1919—25", in: *Problems of Restoration*, Moscow, 1926, vol. 1 (Igor Grabar, *Early Russian Art*, Moscow, 1966, pp. 112—208)

GUSAROVA 1979
E. B. Gusarova, "Russian Half-Length Deesis Tiers of the 15th and 16th Centuries (An Attempt at Iconographic Classification)", in: *Sovietskoye Iskusstvoznanie '78/1* (Soviet Art Studies '78/1), Moscow, 1979

IVANOVA, KUKLES, POPOV 1968
I. Ivanova, A. Kukles, G. Popov, *The Rublev Museum of Early Russian Art*, Moscow, 1968

IVANOVA 1969
I. Ivanova, *The Rublev Museum of Early Russian Art*, Moscow, 1969

KONDAKOV 1905
N. P. Kondakov, *The Iconography of God Almighty and Our Saviour Jesus Christ*, St Petersburg, 1905

LAZAREV 1965
V. N. Lazarev, "About the Principles of a Scholarly Catalogue", *Iskusstvo* (Art), 1965, No. 9

LAZAREV 1969
V. N. Lazarev, *Novgorodian Painting*, Moscow, 1969

LAZAREV 1970
V. N. Lazarev, *Russian Medieval Painting. Articles and Studies*, Moscow, 1970

LAZAREV 1983
V. N. Lazarev, *Russian Icon-Painting from Its Beginnings to the Early 16th Century*, Moscow, 1983

NEKRASOV 1900
V. I. Nekrasov, *The Church of the White Trinity in Tver. A Historical and Archaeological Outline*, Tver, 1900

NEKRASOV 1937
A. I. Nekrasov, *Early Russian Visual Art*, Moscow, 1937

NIKOLAYEVA 1969
T. V. Nikolayeva, *The Collection of Early Russian Art at the Zagorsk Museum*, Leningrad, 1969

NIKOLAYEVA 1977
T. V. Nikolayeva, *Early Russian Painting at the Zagorsk Museum*, Moscow, 1977

OLSUFYEV 1920
Yu. A. Olsufyev, *Inventory of Icons of the Trinity-St Sergius Monastery up to the 18th Century and the More Typical Items of the 18th and 19th Centuries*, Sergiyev, 1920

OLSUFYEV 1935
Yu. A. Olsufyev, "Problems of the Forms of Early Russian Painting", *Sovetsky Muzei* (Soviet Museum), 1935, No. 6; 1936, No. 2

PLUGIN 1974
V. A. Plugin, *The World Outlook of Andrei Rublev (Certain Problems). Early Russian Painting as a Historical Source*, Moscow, 1974

POGOZHEVA 1914
L. Pogozheva, "The Church of the White Trinity in Tver", *Svetilnik* (The Lamplight), 1914, No. 8

POKROVSKY 1892
N. Pokrovsky, *The Gospels in Iconographic Monuments, Primarily Byzantine and Russian*, St Petersburg, 1892

POPOV 1969/70
G. V. Popov, "Artistic Links of Tver with Athos (A Processional Icon of Tver Origin of the First Quarter of the 15th Century)", *Starinar*, new series, XX/1969, Belgrade, 1970

POPOV 1970
G. V. Popov, "Roads of the Evolution of Tver Art in the 14th— Early 16th Centuries (Painting, Illumination)", in: *Early Russian Art. The Artistic Culture of Muscovy and Neighbouring Principalities. 14th—16th Centuries*, Moscow, 1970

POPOV 1971
G. V. Popov, "Late Tver Manuscript Illumination", in: *Archaeographic Yearbook for 1970*, Moscow, 1971

POPOV 1973
G. V. Popov, *Artistic Life in Dmitrov in the 15th and 16th Centuries*, Moscow, 1973

POPOV 1975
G. V. Popov, *Painting and Illumination of Muscovy in the Mid-15th to the Early 16th Century*, Moscow, 1975

POPOV 1977
G. V. Popov, "The Kalinin Tier and the Culture of Tver in the Mid-15th Century", *Early Russian Art: Problems and Attributions*, Moscow, 1977

POPOV 1978
G. V. Popov, "14th-Century. Tver Painting and the Paleologue Style", in: *Medieval Art. Russia. Georgia*, Moscow, 1978

POPOV 1979
G. V. Popov, "Icon-Painting", in: G. V. Popov and A. V. Ryndina, *The Painting and Applied Arts of Tver. 14th—16th Centuries*, Moscow, 1979

POPOV 1982
G. V. Popov, "Tver, Byzantium and the Southern Slavs in the 14th and Early 15th Centuries (A Study of Artistic Life in Tver in the 14th and 15th Centuries)", in: *Russo-Balkan Cultural Ties in the Middle Ages*, Sofia, 1982

PORFIRYEV 1890
I. Ya. Porfiryev, *New Testament Apocrypha about Figures and Events on the Basis of Manuscripts in the Solovetsky Library*, St Petersburg, 1890

ROZANOVA 1970
N. Rozanova, *Rostov-Suzdalian Painting from the 12th—16th Centuries*, Moscow, 1970

ROSTOV-SUZDALIAN PAINTING 1967
Catalogue of an Exhibition of the Rostov-Suzdalian School of Painting, introduction by V. I. Antonova, Moscow, 1967

RUBLEV EXHIBITION 1960
Andrei Rublev. 600th Anniversary Jubilee Exhibition. Catalogue, edited and introduced by V. I. Antonova, compiled by E. F. Kamenskaya, M. A. Reformatskaya and N. B. Salko, Moscow, 1960

RUSSIAN MUSEUM. GUIDE 1954
N. G. Porfiridov, "Early Russian Art", in: *The Russian Museum. Guide*, Moscow, 1954, issue 1

RYNDINA 1979
A. V. Ryndina, "Applied and Plastic Arts", in: G. V. Popov and A. V. Ryndina, *The Painting and Applied Arts of Tver. 14th— 16th Centuries*, Moscow, 1979

SALTYKOV 1981
A. A. Saltykov, *The Rublev Museum of Early Russian Art*, Leningrad, 1981

SERGEYEV 1977
V. N. Sergeyev, "New Discoveries in the Rublev Museum", *Pamiatniki Otechestva* (Motherland Monuments), Moscow, 1977, issue 3

SERGIUS 1876
Archimandrite Sergius, *The Complete Calendar of the East*, Moscow, 1876, vol. 2, parts 1—3

SEVENTH EXHIBITION 1975
Seventh Exhibition of Works of Fine Art Restored at the Grabar Workshops During 1944—74. Catalogue, Moscow, 1975

SIXTH EXHIBITION 1969
Sixth Exhibition of Works of Fine Art Restored at the Grabar Workshops. Catalogue, Moscow, 1969

SMIRNOVA 1976
E. S. Smirnova, *The Painting of Novgorod the Great. Mid-13th — Early 15th Centuries*, Moscow, 1976

SMIRNOVA 1983
E. S. Smirnova, V. K. Laurina, E. A. Gorrodian Manuscripts", in: *Drevnerusskoye Iskusstvo* (Early Russian Art): *Rukopisnaya Kniga* (The Manuscript Book). 3, Moscow, 1983

SMIRNOVA, LAURINA, GORDIYENKO 1982
E. S. Smirnova, V. K. Laurina, E. A. Gordiyenko, *The Painting of Novgorod the Great. 15th Century*, Moscow, 1982

TVER PAINTING 1970
Painting of Ancient Tver. The Rublev Museum of Early Russian Art, Exhibition Catalogue, introduction by L. M. Yevseyeva, Moscow, 1970

USSR. RUSSIAN ICONS 1958
USSR. Early Russian Icons, preface by I. Grabar. Introduction by V. Lazarev and O. Demus, UNESCO, 1958

VAGNER, KUKLES, TIKHOMIROVA 1972
G. K. Vagner, A. S. Kukles, K. G. Tikhomirova, *The Andronicus Monastery of the Saviour. The Andrei Rublev Museum Preserve*, Moscow, 1972

VAGNER 1974
G. K. Vagner, *The Problem of Genre in Early Russian Art*, Moscow, 1974

VLADISLAVLEV 1863
V. Vladislavlev, "Brief Historical Notes about the Monasteries and More Remarkable Churches of the City of Tver", in: *Tver Province Handbook for 1863*, Tver, 1863

VORONIN, LAZAREV 1955
N. N. Voronin, V. N. Lazarev, "Art of the Central Russian Principalities. 13th—15th Centuries", in: *The History of Russian Art*, vol. 3, Moscow, 1955

VZDORNOV 1970
G. I. Vzdornov, "Painting", in: *Essays on Russian Culture of the 13th to 15th Centuries*, Moscow, 1970. Part 2: *Spiritual Culture*

YAGODOVSKAYA 1958
A. Yagodovskaya, "Certain Specific Aspects of the Representation of Reality in Muscovite Icon-Painting of the Turn of the 15th Century", in: *The State Tretyakov Gallery. Materials and Studies*, Moscow, 1958, issue 2

YEVSEYEVA 1981
L. M. Yevseyeva, "The 15th—Century Icons of the Saviour from Vesiegonsk and the Apostle Paul from Chamerovo", in: *Early Russian Art of the 15th—17th Centuries*, Moscow, 1981

YEVSEYEVA, KOCHETKOV, SERGEYEV 1974 (Idem 1983)
L. M. Yevseyeva, I. A. Kochetkov, V. N. Sergeyev, *Painting of Ancient Tver*, Moscow, 1974 (Idem, 2nd edition, revised and enlarged, Moscow, 1983)

ZHIZNEVSKY 1888
A. K. Zhiznevsky, *The Description of the Tver Museum*, with commentaries by A. S. Uvarov, Moscow, 1888

Foreign Sources
ALPATOW 1958; 1962
M. Alpatow, *Altrussische Ikonenmalerei*, Dresden, 1958 (2nd ed., 1962)

ANCIENT RUSSIAN ICONS 1929
Ancient Russian Icons from the XIIth to the XIXth Centuries, London, 1929

L'ART RUSSE DES SCYTHES À NOS JOURS 1967
L'art russe des Scythes à nos jours. Tresors des musées soviétiques. Grand Palais. October 1967 — January 1968, Paris, 1967

CATALOGUE OF RUSSIAN ICONS 1931
Catalogue of Russian Icons Lent by the American Russian Institute, Chicago, 1931

DENKMÄLER ALTRUSSISCHER MALEREI 1929
Denkmäler altrussischer Malerei. Russische Ikonen vom 12.—18. Jahrhundert. Ausstellung, Berlin — Königsberg, 1929

DJOROVIĆ-LUBINCOVIĆ. 1965
M. Djorović-Lubincović, *Srednevekovni duborez i istochnim oblastima Yugoslavii*, Belgrade, 1965 (in Serbian)

DUFRENNE 1972
S. Dufrenne, "Quelques aspects de l'iconographie des peintures de Mistra au temps du despotate de Morée", *Moravska shkola i nieno doba. Nauchni skup u Resavi, 1968*, Belgrade, 1972

LAFONTAINE-DOSOGNE 1964—1965
J. Lafontaine-Dosogne, *Iconographie de l'enfance de la Vierge dans l'Empire Byzantin et en Occident*, 1—2, Brussels, 1964—1965

LAFONTAINE-DOSOGNE 1975
J. Lafontaine-Dosogne, "Iconography of the Cycle the *Life of the Virgin*", *The Kariye Djami*, 4. Ed. P. A. Underwood, Princeton, 1975

LEXIKON 1968—1976
Lexikon der christlichen Ikonographie. Herausgegeben von E. Kirschbaum, vol. 1—8, Rome — Freiburg — Basel — Vienna, 1968—1976

MALARSTWO ROSYJSKIE XIV—XX w. 1957
Malarstwo rosyjskie XIV—XX w. Wystawka w Museum narodowym, Warsaw, 1957

ONASCH 1961
K. Onasch, *Ikonen*, Berlin, 1961

REALLEXIKON 1963—1978
Reallexikon zur byzantinische Kunst. Herausgegeben von K. Wessel. Unter Mitwirkung M. Restle, vol. I—V (issue 1—34), Stuttgart, 1963—1991

SCHWEINFURTH 1930
Ph. Schweinfurth, *Geschichte der russischen Malerei im Mittelalter*, The Hague, 1930

ТВЕРСКАЯ ИКОНА XIII—XVII ВЕКОВ

Альбом (на английском языке)

Издательство «Аврора». Санкт-Петербург. 1993
Изд. № 1111. (С-35)

ГПП им. Ивана Федорова, Санкт-Петербург
Printed and bound in Russia